Praise for

What [A]
Mothe[r]
Don't T[alk]
About

· · · · · · · · ·

Most Anticipated Reads of 2019 Selection by *Publishers Weekly*
BuzzFeed *The Rumpus* *Lit Hub* **and** *O: The Oprah Magazine*

A Best Book of the Year Selection from *Paste* **magazine**
Entropy **and** *Library Journal*

"Each essay is a complete experience in itself, with its own arc and epiphany. . . . Filgate has done a magnificent job of gathering pieces written with love and passion."

—*Los Angeles Review of Book*s

"[A] poignant collection of meditations on what it means to be someone's child, at once raw, comic, and revelatory."

—Esquire.com

"Astonishing . . . These collected essays are variously rich, tender, angry, despairing, and clinical. The result, greater than the sum of parts, is part paean and part denunciation, intelligent, heartfelt, and wise. *What My Mother and I Don't Talk About* is a shrewd, glinting collection of beauty and pain: a gift for mothers and their children."
—*Shelf Awareness*

"By turns joyously heartwarming and plaintively forlorn, a dynamic cast of essayists—Kiese Laymon and Leslie Jamison among them—riff on the women who are 'our first homes' and the lies that 'make fools of the people we love.'"
—*O: The Oprah Magazine*

"These essays, each one exceptional on its own, encompass both love and writing at their most vulnerable, and could power entire cities with their electricity."
—*Booklist*, starred review

"Fifteen essayists—many luminaries—write unflinchingly about their mothers . . . Each one of these intimate and gut-wrenching essays reaches beyond itself to forge connections with readers."
—*Kirkus Reviews*, starred review

"The essays all address the authors' relationships with their mothers in stories to be savored. . . . Beautifully composed."
—*Library Journal*, starred review

"A fascinating set of reflections on what it is like to be a son or daughter.... The range of stories and styles represented in this collection makes for rich and rewarding reading."

—*Publishers Weekly*

"These are the hardest stories in the world to tell, but they are told with absolute grace. You will devour these beautifully written—and very important—tales of honesty, pain, and resilience."

—Elizabeth Gilbert, *New York Times* bestselling author of *Eat Pray Love*

"By turns raw, tender, bold, and wise, the essays in this anthology explore writers' relationships with their mothers. Kudos to Michele Filgate for this riveting contribution to a vital conversation."

—Claire Messud, bestselling author of *The Burning Girl*

"Fifteen literary luminaries, including Filgate herself, probe how silence is never even remotely golden until it is mined for the haunting truths that lie within our most primal relationships—with our mothers. These essays about love, or the terrifying lack of it, don't just smash the silence; they let the light in, bearing witness with grace, understanding, and writing so gorgeous you'll be memorizing lines."

—Caroline Leavitt, *New York Times* bestselling author of *Is This Tomorrow* and *Pictures of You*

"This collection of storytelling constellated around mothers and silence will break your heart and then gently give it back to you stitched together with what we carry in our bodies our whole lives."

—Lidia Yuknavitch, national bestselling author of *The Misfit's Manifesto*

"This is a rare collection that has the power to break silences. I am in awe of the talent Filgate has assembled here; each of these fifteen heavyweight writers offer a truly profound argument for why words matter, and why unspoken words may matter even more."

—Garrard Conley, *New York Times* bestselling author of *Boy Erased*

"Who better to discuss one of our greatest shared surrealities—that we are all, once and forever, for better or worse, someone's child— than this murderer's row of writers? I'll be thinking about this book, and stewing over it, and teaching from it, for a long time."

—Rebecca Makkai, author of *The Great Believers*

What My Mother and I Don't Talk About

Fifteen Writers Break the Silence

Edited by Michele Filgate

Simon & Schuster Paperbacks

New York   London   Toronto   Sydney   New Delhi

Simon & Schuster Paperbacks
An Imprint of Simon & Schuster, Inc
1230 Avenue of the Americas
New York, NY 10020

Permissions are listed on page 267, which is considered a continuation of this copyright page.

Copyright © 2019 by Michele Filgate

All rights reserved, including the right to reproduce this book or portions thereof in any form whatsoever. For information, address Simon & Schuster Paperbacks Subsidiary Rights Department, 1230 Avenue of the Americas, New York, NY 10020.

First Simon & Schuster trade paperback edition May 2020

SIMON & SCHUSTER PAPERBACKS and colophon are registered trademarks of Simon & Schuster, Inc.

For information about special discounts for bulk purchases, please contact Simon & Schuster Special Sales at 1-866-506-1949 or business@simonandschuster.com.

The Simon & Schuster Speakers Bureau can bring authors to your live event. For more information or to book an event, contact the Simon & Schuster Speakers Bureau at 1-866-248-3049 or visit our website at www.simonspeakers.com.

Interior design by Ruth Lee-Mui

Manufactured in the United States of America

20 19 18 17 16 15 14 13 12 11

Library of Congress Cataloging-in-Publication Data

Names: Filgate, Michele, editor.
Title: What my mother and I don't talk about : Fifteen writers break the silence / edited by Michele Filgate.
Description: New York : Simon & Schuster, [2019] | Includes bibliographical references and index.
Identifiers: LCCN 2018053899 (print) | LCCN 2018057436 (ebook) | ISBN 9781982107369 (ebook) | ISBN 9781982107345 (hardcover : alk. paper) | ISBN 9781982107352 (trade pbk. : alk. paper)
Subjects: LCSH: Mother and child. | Mothers. | Parent and adult child.
Classification: LCC HQ759 (ebook) | LCC HQ759 .W4554 2019 (print) | DDC 306.874/3—dc23
LC record available at https://lccn.loc.gov/2018053899

ISBN 978-1-9821-0734-5
ISBN 978-1-9821-0735-2 (pbk)
ISBN 978-1-9821-0736-9 (ebook)

For Mimo and Nana

Because it is a thousand pities never to say what one feels . . .

—Virginia Woolf, *Mrs. Dalloway*

Contents

Contents

Introduction

by Michele Filgate

On the first cold day of November, when it was so frigid that I finally needed to accept the fact that it was time to take my winter coat out of the closet, I had a craving for something warm and savory. I stopped at the local butcher in my neighborhood in Brooklyn and bought a half pound of bacon and two and a half pounds of chuck beef.

At home, I washed and chopped the mushrooms, removing their stems and feeling some sense of satisfaction as the dirt swirled down the drain. I put on Christmas music, though it wasn't even close to Thanksgiving, and my tiny apartment expanded with a comforting smell: onions, carrots, garlic, and bacon fat simmering on the stove.

Cooking Ina Garten's beef bourguignon is a way I feel close to my mother. Stirring the fragrant stew, I'm back in my childhood kitchen, where my mother would spend a good chunk of her time when she wasn't at work. Around the holiday season, she'd bake poppy seed cookies with raspberry jam in the middle, or peanut butter blossoms, and I'd help her with the dough.

As I'm making the meal, I feel my mother's presence in the room. I can't cook without thinking of her, because the kitchen is where she feels most at home. Adding the beef stock and fresh thyme, I'm reassured by the simple act of creation. If you use the right ingredients and follow the directions, something emerges that pleases your palate. Still, by the end of the night, despite my full belly I'm left with a gnawing pain in my stomach.

My mother and I don't speak that often. Making a recipe is a contract with myself that I can execute easily. Talking to my mother isn't as simple, nor was writing my essay in this book.

It took me twelve years to write the essay that led to this anthology. When I first started writing "What My Mother and I Don't Talk About," I was an undergraduate at the University of New Hampshire, wowed by Jo Ann Beard's influential essay collection *The Boys of My Youth*. Reading that book was the first instance that showed me what a personal essay can really be: a place where a writer can lay claim for control over their own story. At the time, I was full of anger toward my abusive stepfather, haunted by memories that were all too recent. He loomed so large in my house that I wanted to disappear until, finally, I did.

What I didn't realize at the time was that this essay wasn't *really* about my stepfather. The reality was far more complicated and difficult to face. The core truths behind my essay took years to confront and articulate. What I wanted (and needed) to write about was my fractured relationship with my mother.

Longreads published my essay in October 2017, right after the Weinstein story broke and the #MeToo movement took off. It was the perfect time to break my silence, but the morning it was published, I woke up early at a friend's house in Sausalito, unable to sleep, rattled by how it felt to release such a vulnerable piece of writing into the world. The sun was just rising as I sat outside and opened my laptop. The air was thick with smoke from nearby wildfires, and ash rained down on my keyboard. It felt like the whole world was burning. It felt like I had set fire to my own life. To live with the pain of my strained relationship with my mother is one thing. To immortalize it in words is a whole other level.

There's something deeply lonely about confessing your truth. The thing was, I wasn't truly alone. For even a brief instant of time, every single human being has a mother. That mother-and-child connection is a complicated one. Yet we live in a society where we have holidays that assume a happy relationship. Every year when Mother's Day rolls around, I brace myself for the onslaught of Facebook posts paying tribute to the strong, loving women who shaped their offspring. I'm always happy to see mothers celebrated, but there's a part of me that finds it painful too. There is a huge swath of people who are reminded on this day of what is lacking in their lives—for some, it's the intense grief that comes with losing a mother too soon or never even knowing her. For others, it's the realization that their mother, although alive, doesn't know how to mother them.

Mothers are idealized as protectors: a person who is caring and giving and who builds a person up rather than knocking them down. But very few of us can say that our mothers check all of these boxes. In many ways, a mother is set up to fail. "There is a gaping hole perhaps for all of us, where our mother does not match up with 'mother' as we believe it's meant to mean and all it's meant to give us," Lynn Steger Strong writes in this book.

That gap can be a normal and necessary experience of reality as we grow—it can also leave a lasting effect. Just as every human being has a mother, we all share the instinct to avoid pain at all costs. We try to bury it deep inside of us until we can no longer feel it, until we forget that it exists. This is how we survive. But it's not the *only* way.

There's a relief in breaking the silence. This is also how we grow. Acknowledging what we couldn't say for so long, for whatever reason, is one way to heal our relationships with others and, perhaps most important, with ourselves. But doing this as a community is much easier than standing alone on a stage.

While some of the fourteen writers in this book are estranged from their mothers, others are extremely close. Leslie Jamison writes: "To talk about her love for me, or mine for her, would feel almost tautological; she has always defined my notion of what love is." Leslie attempts to understand who her mother was before she became her mom by reading the unpublished novel written by her mother's ex-husband. In Cathi Hanauer's hilarious piece, she finally gets a chance to have a conversation with her mother that isn't interrupted by her domineering (but lovable) father. Dylan Landis wonders if the friendship between her mother and the painter Haywood Bill Rivers ran deeper than she revealed. André Aciman writes about what it was like to have a deaf mother. Melissa Febos uses mythology as a lens to look at her close-knit relationship with her psychotherapist mother. And Julianna Baggott talks about having a mom who tells her *everything*. Sari Botton writes about her mother becoming something of a "class traitor" after her economic status changed, and the ways in which giving and receiving became complicated between them.

There's a solid river of deep pain that runs throughout this book too. Brandon Taylor writes with astonishing tenderness about a mother who verbally and physically abused him. Nayomi Munaweera shares what it's like to grow up in a chaotic household colored by immigration, mental illness, and domestic abuse. Carmen Maria Machado examines her ambivalence about parenthood being linked to her estranged relationship with her mother. Alexander Chee examines the mistaken responsibility he felt to shield his mother from the sexual abuse he received as a child. Kiese Laymon tells his mother why he wrote his memoir for her: "I know, after finishing this project, the problem in this country is not that we fail to 'get along' with people, parties, and politics with which we disagree. The problem is that we are horrific at justly loving the people, places, and politics we purport to love. I wrote *Heavy* to you because I wanted us to get better at love." And Bernice L. McFadden writes about how false accusations can linger within families for decades.

My hope for this book is that it will serve as a beacon for anyone who has ever felt incapable of speaking their truth or their mother's truth. The more we face what we can't or won't or don't know, the more we understand one another.

I long for the mother I had before she met my stepfather, but also the mother she still was even after she married him. Sometimes I imagine what it would be like to give this book to my mother. To present it to her as a precious gift over a meal that I've cooked for her. To say: Here is everything that keeps us from really talking. Here is my heart. Here are my words. I wrote this for you.

What My Mother and I Don't Talk About

By Michele Filgate

*L*acuna: *an unfilled space or interval, a gap.*

Our mothers are our first homes, and that's why we're always trying to return to them. To know what it was like to have one place where we belonged. Where we fit.

My mother is hard to know. Or rather, I know her and don't know her at the same time. I can imagine her long, grayish-brown hair that she refuses to chop off, the vodka and ice in her hand. But if I try to conjure her face, I'm met instead by her laugh, a fake laugh, the kind of laugh that is trying to prove something, a forced happiness.

Several times a week, she posts tempting photos of food on her Facebook page. Achiote pork tacos with pickled red onions, strips of beef jerky just out of the smoker, slabs of steak that she serves with steamed vegetables. These are the meals of my childhood—sometimes ambitious and sometimes practical. But these meals, for me, call to mind my stepfather: the red of his face, the red of the blood pooled on the plate. He uses a dish towel to wipe the sweat from his cheeks; his work boots are coated in sawdust. His words puncture me, tines of a fork stuck in a half-deflated balloon.

You are the one causing problems in my marriage, he says. *You fucking bitch*, he says. *I'll slam you*, he says. And I'm afraid he will; I'm afraid he'll press himself on top of me on my bed until the mattress opens up and swallows me whole. Now, my mother saves all of her cooking skills for her husband. Now, she serves him food at their farmhouse in the country and their condo in the city. Now, my mother no longer cooks for me.

My teenage bedroom is covered in centerfolds from *Teen Beat* and faded ink-jet printouts of Leonardo DiCaprio and Jakob Dylan. Dog-fur tumbleweeds float around when a breeze comes through my front window. No matter how much my mother vacuums, they multiply.

My desk is covered in a mess of textbooks and half-written letters and uncapped pens and dried-up highlighters and pencils sharpened to slivers. I write sitting on the hardwood floor, my back pressed against the hard red knobs of my dresser. It isn't comfortable, but something about the constant pressure grounds me.

I write terrible poems that I think, in a moment of teenage vanity, are quite brilliant. Poems about heartbreak and being misunderstood and being inspired. I print them out on paper with a sunset beach scene in the background and name the collection *Summer's Snow*.

While I write, my stepfather sits at his desk that's right outside my bedroom. He's working on his laptop, but every time his chair squeaks or he makes any kind of movement, fear rises up from my stomach to the back of my throat. I keep my door closed, but that's useless, since I'm not allowed to lock it.

Shortly after my stepfather married my mother, he made a simple jewelry box for me that sits on top of my dresser. The wood is smooth and glossy. No nicks or grooves in the surface. I keep broken necklaces and gaudy bracelets in it. Things I want to forget.

Like those baubles in the box, I can play with existing and not existing inside my bedroom; my room is a place to be myself and not myself. I disappear into books like they are black holes. When I can't focus, I lie for hours on my bottom bunk bed, waiting for my boyfriend to call and save me from my thoughts. Save me from my mother's husband. The phone doesn't ring. The silence cuts me. I grow moodier. I shrink inside of myself, stacking sadness on top of anxiety on top of daydreaming.

"What are the two things that make the world go 'round?" My stepfather is asking me a question he always asks. We are in his woodworking shop in the basement, and he's wearing his boots and an old pair of jeans with a threadbare T-shirt. He smells like whiskey.

I know what the answer is. I know it, but I do not want to say it. He is staring at me expectantly, his skin crinkled around half-shut eyes, his boozy breath hot on my face.

"Sex and money," I grumble. The words feel like hot coals in my mouth, heavy and shame-ridden.

"That's right," he says. "Now, if you're extra, extra nice to me, maybe I can get you into that school you want to go to."

He knows my dream is to go to SUNY Purchase for acting. When I am on the stage, I am transformed and transported into a life that isn't my own. I am someone with even bigger problems, but problems that might be resolved by the end of an evening.

I want to leave the basement. But I can't just walk away from him. I'm not allowed to do that.

The exposed light bulb makes me feel like a character in a noir film. The air is colder, heavier down here. I think back to a year before, when he parked his truck in front of the ocean and put his hand on my inner thigh, testing me, seeing how far he could go. I insisted he drive me home. He wouldn't, for at least a long, excruciating half hour. When I told my mom, she didn't believe me.

Now he is up against me, arms coiled around my back. The tines of the fork return, this time letting all the air out. He talks softly in my ear.

"This is just between you and me. Not your mother. Understand?"

I don't understand. He pinches my ass. He is hugging me in a way that stepfathers should not hug their stepdaughters. His hands are worms, my body dirt.

I break free from him and run upstairs. Mom is in the kitchen. She's always in the kitchen. "Your husband grabbed my butt," I spit out. She quietly sets down the wooden spoon she is using to stir and goes downstairs. The spoon is stained red with spaghetti sauce.

Later, she finds me curled up in the fetal position in my room. "Don't worry," she says. "He was only joking."

On an afternoon several years earlier, I step down from the school bus. The walk from the end of my block to my driveway is always full of tension. If my stepfather's tomato-red pickup truck is in the driveway, it means I have to be in the house with him. But today there is no truck. I am alone. Deliciously alone. And on the counter, a coffee cake my mother baked, the crumbled brown sugar making my mouth water. I cut into it and devour half of the dessert in a couple of bites. My tongue begins to tingle, the first sign of an anaphylactic reaction. I'm used to them. I know what to do: take liquid Benadryl right away and let the artificial-cherry syrup coat my tongue as it puffs up like a fish, blocking my airway. My throat starts to close.

But we only have pills. They take a lot longer to dissolve. I swallow them and immediately throw up. My breath comes only in squeaky gasps. I run to the beige phone on the wall. Dial 911. The minutes it takes the EMTs to arrive are as long as my thirteen years on Earth. I stare into the mirror at my tearstained face, trying to stop crying because it makes it even harder to breathe. The tears come anyway.

In the ambulance on the way to the emergency room, they give me a teddy bear. I hold it close to me like a newborn baby.

Later, my mother pushes the curtain aside and steps next to my hospital bed. She's frowning and relieved at the same time. "There were crushed walnuts on the top of that cake. I baked it for a coworker," she says. She looks at the teddy bear still cradled in my arms. "I forgot to leave a note for you."

I've spent enough time in Catholic churches to know what it means to sweep things underneath the rug. My family is good at that, until we're not. Sometimes our secrets are still partially visible. It's easy to trip over them.

The silence in the church isn't always peaceful. It just makes it more jarring when the tiniest noise, a muffled cough or a creaky knee, echoes throughout the sanctuary. You can't be wholly yourself there. You have to hollow yourself out, like a husk.

In high school, I'm the opposite. I'm too much myself, because the too muchness is a way of saying, *I'm still here. The me of me, and not the me he wants me to be.* Anything can set me off. I run out of biology class multiple times a week, and my teacher follows me to the girls' room, pressing tissues that feel like sandpaper to my cheek. I hang out in the nurse's office whenever I can't handle being around other people.

● ● ●

Here's what silence sounds like after he loses his temper. After I, in a moment of bravery, scream back at him, *You're NOT my father*.

It sounds like an egg cracked once against a porcelain bowl. It sounds like the skin of an orange, peeled away from the fruit. It sounds like a muffled sneeze in church.

Good girls are quiet.

Bad girls kneel on uncooked rice, the hard pellets digging into their exposed knees. Or at least that's what I'm told by a former coworker who went to an all-girls Catholic school in Brooklyn. The nuns preferred this kind of corporal punishment.

Good girls don't disrupt the class.

Bad girls visit the guidance counselor so frequently that she keeps an extra supply of tissues just for them. Bad girls talk to the police officer who is assigned to their high school. They roll the tissues in their hands until they crumble like a muffin.

Good girls look anywhere but in the police officer's eyes. They stare at the second hand on the clock mounted on the wall. They tell the officer, "No, it's okay. You don't need to talk to my stepfather and mother. It will just make things worse."

Silence is what fills the gap between my mother and me. All of the things we haven't said to each other, because it's too painful to articulate.

What I want to say: *I need you to believe me. I need you to listen. I need you.*

What I say: nothing.

Nothing until I say everything. But articulating what happened isn't enough. She's still married to him. The gap widens.

My mother sees ghosts. She always has. We're on Martha's Vineyard, and I'm stuck at home with my younger brother—a de facto babysitter while the adults go out for fried clams and drinks. It's an unusually cool August night and the air is so still, like it's holding its breath. I'm next to my brother on the bed, trying to get him to fall asleep. Suddenly I hear someone, some-*thing*, exhale in my ear. The ear turned away from my brother. The windows are closed. No one else is there. I shriek and jump off of the bed.

When my mother walks through the door, I tell her right away.

"You've always had an overactive imagination, Mish," she says, and laughs it off, like a wave temporarily covering jagged shells on the beach.

But a few nights after we leave the island, she confides in me.

"I woke up one night and someone was sitting on my chest," she says. "I didn't want to tell you while we were there. I didn't want to scare you."

I sit in my writing spot on the floor in my bedroom that night, the red knobs of the dresser pressing into my spine, and I think about my mother's ghosts, about her face, about home. Where the TV is always on, and food is always on the table. Where dinners are ruined when I'm at the table, so my stepfather says I have to eat on my own. Where a vase is thrown, the shattering like soft but sharp music on the hardwood floor. Where my stepfather's guns are displayed behind a glass case, and his handgun is hidden underneath a stack of shirts in the closet. Where I crawl on my knees through the pine trees, picking up dog shit. Where there's a pool, but neither my mother nor I know how to do anything more than doggy-paddle.

Where my stepfather makes me a box, and my mother teaches me how to keep my secrets inside.

Now I buy my own Benadryl and keep it on me at all times. These days, my mother and I mostly communicate via group text messages along with my older sister, in which my mother and I reply to my sister, who shares photos of my niece and nephews. Joey in his Cozy Coupe, grinning at the camera while he holds on to the wheel.

One day, I tried to reach out.

I'm going to Nana's this weekend. Maybe you can come down and visit me while I'm there?

She didn't respond.

I text rather than call her because she might be in the same room as him. I like to pretend he doesn't exist. And I'm good at it. She taught me. Like with the broken baubles in my old jewelry box, I just close the lid.

I wait for a text reply from her, some excuse about why she can't get away. When Nana picks me up from the train station, I secretly hope my mother is in the car with her, wanting to surprise me.

I check my messages and think about disjointed collages I used to piece together out of old *National Geographic*s, *Family Circle*s, and Sears catalogs; an advertisement for Campbell's tomato soup pasted next to a leopard, attached next to half of a headline, like "Ten Tips for." Even as a child, I was comforted by the not-finishing, the nonsensicalness of the collages. They made me feel like anything was possible. All you had to do was begin.

Her car never appeared in the driveway. A message never appeared on my phone.

My mother's farmhouse, two hours away from my hometown, was built by a Revolutionary War soldier with his own hands. It's haunted, of course. Several years ago, she posted a photo on Facebook of the backyard, lush and green, with tiny orbs appearing like starlight.

"I love you past the sun and the moon and the stars," she'd always say to me when I was little. But I just want her to love me here. Now. On Earth.

My Mother's (Gate) Keeper

By Cathi Hanauer

In a way, this is a story of love. One version of love, anyway. For better and worse.

First, the prologue.

My mother and father met, in 1953, at a party in South Orange, New Jersey, at the home of someone named Merle Ann Beck. My mother, a high school junior, knew her vaguely, and my father not at all, but long story short, they both made the list. Hearing that list, my mother liked my father's name, Lonnie Hanauer—something about all those smooth-sounding *n*s. She asked about him and learned that although he was only seventeen months her senior—she was sixteen and a half, he newly eighteen—he was already a sophomore at Cornell, pre-med. She was intrigued, and though she was a quiet, studious "good girl" who helped lay out the school paper and sometimes worked in her father's dry-goods store, she sought him out at the party. They talked and danced; she found him sophisticated and funny. Later that night, she told her mother she'd met the man she would marry.

Three years and eight months later, at his family's country club—pristine blue pool and a golf course that rivaled those of the WASP-y clubs nearby—she did just that. He was twenty-one and a half. She had just turned twenty.

That was sixty-one years, four children, and six grandchildren ago. I am the oldest of those children, and the one who, it seems, is always looking for answers, especially about my mother.

Ten or so years ago, when I was in my forties and my parents just over seventy, my mother got her own email address. This might not seem like a big deal, but in her case, it was huge. Before that, since the days of AOL and "You've got mail!" my parents had shared an email address. So did many of their friends, couples who didn't have the internet or email until their sixties and probably thought, at least at first, that it was similar to sharing a regular mail address or a land phone line. But unlike most other couples, when people emailed my mother—her daughters, her best friend, her brothers—my father not only read the message but also often answered it. Sometimes my mother answered, too, and sometimes not. She seemed to think this was how it worked.

The same dynamic was true with phone calls. When you

called the house, my father answered. As you said hello, he'd yell, "Bette! Pick up!" and then the click, and she was on, too. I learned long ago that if I asked to speak to my mother, he'd say, "She's listening. Go ahead"; if I said that I meant *privately*, he'd say something along the lines of, "Whatever you tell her, you can tell me." It didn't matter if I pleaded or reasoned or raged; he stayed on. Then he often talked for her. If you asked, "How do you feel, Mom?" after she'd been sick, he might say, "She feels good. Her fever is gone and she just had some toast." If you then said, "I asked *Mom* how she feels. Mom, how do you feel?" she'd offer something innocuous and upbeat: "I'm much better," or "I'm fine."

If you asked about something specifically female that a daughter might ask her mother—how she first knew she was pregnant, what to give someone for their wedding, how to make her famous blueberry tart—often *he* would respond, even if he didn't know the answer. "She makes it with apricot preserves. Right, Bette?" Or: "It's crass to give money; buy something, so they remember you when they use it." If he truly had nothing to say—if you asked her, say, about a book she was reading—he might turn up the baseball game on TV, then comment on it loudly: "Goddamn it, Martinez! Catch the fucking ball!" Or he'd tell you what he and my mother had done the past few days—dinners out, movies—and then give you his opinion of those events. "Have you seen X yet?" he'd ask, and if I said no, he'd say, "I gave it three stars." (His top rating is four.) He'd then tell you how cute the adolescent female lead was and, finally, a spoiler about the end. When I complained, he'd say, "Hamlet dies at the end, too, you know."

This, his phone and email behavior, for starters—combined with my mother's enduring it all without a peep—was a frustrating mystery to me. Didn't she consider this an invasion of her privacy, or realize how annoying it was to others? If so, why didn't she speak up? There were other egregious things, too. When, with a carful of people, he drove like he was on the lam in a game of *Grand Theft Auto*, whipping around speed bumps, blowing through stop signs, blaring his horn at anyone in his way. Or when he caused a scene on their trip to a national park because he didn't like the tour—too much birding, not enough hiking—until finally he had to be escorted back to headquarters, my mother in tow, while everyone else waited.

When he yelled at her if she fed the dog when he'd wanted to, or, ever thrifty, ate leftovers while serving him a fresh meal she'd just made (he didn't like it when she deprived herself). Sometimes, especially on the phone, his whole act was so unbelievable—so comically obnoxious, like a parody of itself—that I actually laughed. I'd say, "Thank you for telling me how *Mom* feels / thinks / makes her blueberry tart." Then he'd laugh, and then she'd laugh, too, in that way she always does when someone makes fun of her, which is how you show affection in my family. He'll laugh when he reads this—which he will, since he reads everything I write, generously and proudly. Being able to be criticized—made fun of, even—is one of his admirable qualities. Also, though, he has no shame about any of these actions. "Why should I?" he would say. "I'm a safe driver, and that tour guide was a jerk. And your mother shouldn't eat so many leftovers."

I spent decades trying to fight my father's behavior, first toward me, later toward both me and my mother—his temper and volatility, narcissism, need to control and dominate—but also trying to get access to my mother, to be with or even talk to her without him in the way. This was not only because I wanted to understand her, and her relationship with him, but also, admittedly, because I wanted a piece of her, too; she was my mother, after all! My tiny, gentle, silver-haired, gardening, cooking, dog-walking, composting, eighty-one-year-old mother, who has WELCOME! signs in her garden and pictures of her grandchildren on every refrigerator inch, who reads and critiques all my writing, who never forgets a birthday or anniversary and sends a card featuring a photo she once took of the recipient; who's devoted her life to teaching children with disabilities along with raising her own four; who always remembers to ask about *you*. Who wouldn't want some of that? As a child I shared her with my first sister, along with my father, from the time I was nineteen months old; by the time my second sister came along, and then my brother, she was never without a gaggle of kids and dogs as she bustled about, food shopping, carpooling, making macaroni and cheese and waffles, leading Brownie troops and sewing us Halloween costumes or matching pink-and-white-checked maxiskirts. She did not lounge, or "lunch," or have coffee or cigarettes or afternoon cocktails. She ran around, tending to everyone's needs, until my father came home, and then she tended to his.

For a long time after I grew up, I had no more access to my mother than I'd had as a kid, and probably less. I had moved to Manhattan after college, and when I went back to visit my parents in New Jersey—an evening after work, a weekend every couple of months—my father was always either there or on the way home. Sometimes my mother and I had a few minutes before he arrived, but then the garage door cracked open and his white Mercedes sailed in, radio blaring an opera or the news, and my mother rose to get ready. Or later, in the kitchen, she and I might clean up together while he read or watched TV in the den. But soon he'd come in to read her an article, or he'd call her to watch something on TV. He seemed unable to be without her—or maybe he just didn't want to leave her with me, a feisty, self-supporting feminist saying things that he probably felt threatened the status quo in his house.

Did she mind that he picked all their Friday-night movies or Sunday TV, demanding that she watch with him? As a woman who has always needed autonomy in my own relationships and marriage, I could not imagine feeling, always, so *required*. (I would think of that song from *Oliver!*: "As long as he needs me / I know where I must be.") But it also frustrated me, the constant claims on her time. I'd think, "What about me?" Though sometimes I also thought, "Maybe she doesn't *want* to hang out with me." After all, I can be intense, talky, opinionated, too, like my father—though, as a reasonably self-aware female and mother, also very different. I like to ask questions, to dig deep. *Are you happy with your life? If you could change one thing, what would it be?* But my youngest sister, who's less talky and probing, also sometimes felt this way about my mother: unsure of what she wanted. Was it us? Her? Him? She was a mystery.

By the time my mother got her private email address, I had been communicating with my parents by email for a long time, having found this the best way to talk to my father. I was in my thirties when email became popular, with two young children and a living to make, and I could write my parents when I had time and privacy. Plus, email traded the stress of listening to my father on the phone for the relative ease of reading what he said, which I often liked—he is intelligent, sometimes funny, and up on everything: news, politics, entertainment. If he knows you're interested in something, he'll find articles and send them to you. Same, though, if he knows that something offends you. "That bitch Mattress Girl just wanted attention. If she hadn't, she wouldn't have—" Delete! Done, without having to put my mother in between us.

This pissed him off, my switching from phone calls to email—it took away his ability to hold forth loudly, with both my and my mother's attention—and for years he protested, but by then, thank you every therapist I've ever had, I didn't care or back down. But when my mother got her own address—something he also protested once he found out (and he didn't right away), but that, surprisingly, she held firm on . . . well, that seemed to be a game changer.

While I had long understood my father by this point, my mother still baffled me. Who was she, beyond the energetic, green-eyed teacher, tutor, friendly neighbor who, despite being barely five foot one and ninety pounds soaking wet, lived on black coffee and thin cheese sandwiches, one tablespoonful of yogurt each morning with exactly two walnuts on top? Beyond the woman who dutifully got into bed every night with my father but hours later snuck into my late brother's room to read novel after novel? What were her dreams—or did she not have any, beyond the comfortable, practical, admirable life she was living? Kids and grandkids who loved her, a lively dog from a shelter, a tidy, well-maintained house and garden, a position on the board of the school that she'd helped build from the ground up. A marriage that had lasted more than six decades, enough money to age comfortably. Did she think about my brother, adopted at six weeks old because my parents (my father?) had wanted a fourth child and a boy, and who had died in his thirties, following a troubled young life, after a horrifying accident caused by drug use and inebriation? Did she have regrets? What would she change about her life, if she could change anything?

I could *ask* her now, along with this: Why didn't she protest my father's bad behavior, to her and her children and others? Or did she think there wasn't actually a problem, and I was just oversensitive? (I know how my father would answer that.) When he'd smacked me, hard, in the face, in fourth grade because he overheard me use a word I didn't even realize was forbidden; when he shoved my adolescent sister a little too hard and she plummeted—oops!—down the steps (She was fine! We had carpeting!); when he ridiculed me about my verbal SAT score (something he still does today, despite my longtime career as a novelist, editor, writer) . . . should I simply have ignored it and moved on, as my mother did?

My father had arbitrary rules for a girl who got good grades, didn't get shit-face drunk, even helped run his medical office (he wouldn't let me have any other job): I could go to the movies with my friends or boyfriend, but only to see films *he* deemed intellectual enough—so if a group of my fifteen-year-old friends was going to see, say, *Halloween*, or *Jaws 2*, I had to make them see *The Deer Hunter* instead, or I couldn't go. Did my mother, my other guardian, *agree* with this parenting? He wasn't beating me, starving me, kicking me out, but still: Why the hell didn't she open her mouth? As a teenager I was too enraged to ask her calmly, though when I'd wail, "Why don't you tell him to stop *doing* that?!" she wouldn't, or couldn't, or at any rate *didn't*, say a word, no matter how I begged. Was she complicit? Afraid? As an adult, and with—finally!—direct access to her, I could get answers.

But access, I soon found, didn't give me much more insight than I already had—at least not right away. Sometimes she simply didn't respond when I asked about my father; other times she emailed back briefly, her answers short, unrevealing—at least to my mind. "I can't control him," she'd say, when I asked why she allowed him to throw a full, screaming tantrum on Thanksgiving because someone ate the last shrimp on the platter, even though there were more right in the kitchen. "It doesn't matter what I tell him," she would say, or, "If I ask him to stop, he just gets angry." These all were and are true, but could you *ignore* such behavior from your husband? His grandchildren's mouths dropped, before they went off to whisper and giggle (to be fair, they found him hilarious). Why didn't she speak up? Give an ultimatum? Though what that might be, I couldn't imagine.

What my email relationship with my mother did do was provide a way to talk to her that was *fun*.

Now if I asked a question about child-rearing or a recipe, she could answer it, all by herself. She'd tell me about a new kid she was tutoring, or about visiting a museum in the city with her oldest friend; going alone to New York was something she'd only begun doing in the past decade or so. She told me the history of her family. And we talked about books, now without anyone on the extension asking where the hell the letter opener was. My mother loves almost any novel, unless there's "too much" smoking, drinking, swearing, or adultery. She began to follow the careers of my writer friends and to invite some of them, as she had me, to her book clubs. "I *love* your mother!" they would tell me, after busing to her house for egg salad and coffee with her peers, fresh-cut hydrangeas from her garden decorating the table. They liked my father, too, who picked them up at the bus stop, friendly and joking, turning on the charm and chivalry he calls up when he wants to. He reads books, too—and not just male writers, either. Among his favorites are *Pride and Prejudice* and *Middlemarch*. Four stars each.

But what my mother still didn't do in our new email correspondence, at least not often or with depth, was self-analyze or discuss my father's behavior—toward her, toward me, or in the world—in a way that made me understand what she thought about it. Sometimes she laughed or gently made fun of me for asking. ("Oh, Cathi, I don't know!") And eventually, now that I knew it was *her* choice not to talk about all this, or maybe just because I never got very far, I backed off—a little, at least. When I visited my parents, I tried to stay out of their relationship, though sometimes I failed. "Stop yelling at her!" I'd yell, when he exploded about the stupid fucking shrimp, or his pounds of cashews from Costco that someone dared help themselves to—and sometimes, now, he actually listened; it didn't hurt that there were suddenly four mature granddaughters along with three adult daughters to jump on the *Girl Power* ship, his two mild-mannered grandsons, with their feminist mothers, cheering on their sisters and cousins. He was outnumbered. Sometimes I even felt sorry for him; another straight white man being #MeToo'd at his own dinner table. After all, if it weren't for him, none of us would be here—in this room, or anywhere at all.

And overall, we were fine—fine!—in part thanks to him. We had good lives, weren't estranged, got together a few times a year, a healthy, privileged family of thirteen or fourteen ... not so bad, after fifty-five years. I had survived my childhood with him at its helm, and I still chose to engage and spend time with the guy, not just to access my mother, but because sometimes I enjoyed it and I knew he did, too. And because he wasn't getting younger, and because, as always, he was generous in many ways: giving medical advice, taking my kids out to dinner or even on vacation, and, now, helping his grandchildren pay for college (as long as they went to schools he approved of: Cornell was ideal, because he'd gone there, but Brown was not; it was "pretentious"). He had always supported the positives in my life—particularly my work—as much as he'd blasted what he'd perceived as the negatives. He and my mother, the dark-haired, then gray-haired, then white-haired couple on the cruise to Helsinki or Venice or Juneau, handing out cards for my latest book and bragging about my husband's newspaper column. I did not take that for granted.

The next day, though, he'd copy someone into a long personal email exchange between us (I've begged him not to), or comment disturbingly about some young girl's attractiveness or lack thereof (ditto) ... and there we were again. And my mother— my mother, whom this essay is supposed to be about (Do you see what happens here?)—my mother would go silent, almost as if she were condemning me, too. *Was* she? If so, then okay! But I wanted to hear it.

And so, to write this essay, I decided to find out, once and for all. My parents are eighty-two and eighty-one now; they're healthy as horses, but you just never know when it's your last chance to get answers to questions you've had your whole life. So I emailed my mother, saying I'm writing about the things we don't talk about, and would she be willing to, well, talk to me about them. She said yes. We set up a time when my father would be at the hospital, where he still sees patients a few mornings a week. And we got on the phone.

My mother, it seems to me, has changed in the past twenty years, particularly the past ten. After the relentless busyness of so many decades of her life—the mothering, wife-ing, teaching, bookkeeping for my father's practice—she's had time to slow down and branch out. The women's groups, the book groups, the board she's sat on . . . at eighty-one, she's no wallflower. I almost felt she was excited to talk to me; at any rate, I didn't think she minded.

After some small talk, I cut to the chase. "When you two met," I said, "did he have the temper he has now? If not, when did you first notice it?"

"He didn't," she said. "As his life got more complicated, he put a lot of strictures on how he wanted things to be. And when they weren't that way, he got angry." She paused. "But no, his temper didn't come until much later, I think. I *think*. And that's part of why we've stayed married all these years, Cathi—because I forget things quickly. I get very angry at him, and then I forget all about it. But I also didn't, and still don't, analyze marriage or relationships the way your generation does. We were a naïve age, I think."

Fair enough, though great thinkers, from Gloria Steinem to Betty Friedan, Germaine Greer to the brilliant Vivian Gornick (almost exactly my mother's age), also come from her generation. Still, three of those four didn't have children—and yes, I do think that changed things back then: your worldview, your priorities, the power you had, if any, to be independent and therefore outspoken. "Do you agree he was your gatekeeper?" I asked. "That he shielded you from others? Me, your friends, some other family?"

"I think he definitely did, and still does, keep me from . . . like, the teachers at my school. The principal was always trying to organize after-school events, like meeting in a bar, or going out for dinner. And I never wanted to do those things"—here I couldn't help noticing the shift, from what he wanted to what she wanted, seemingly one and the same—"first because I had four kids and a busy life—I kept the books for him all those years, so after dinner I was always running upstairs to write down something he told me, or call the insurance company for a patient." She mentions that her New York friend, who's divorced, would always say, "Come sleep over with me!" She added, "But I don't do things like that."

Me: "Why?"

"Well, I think he *did* keep me for himself. What you say is right. He was, and is, a very demanding person, and he always made me feel that my first obligation was to him. And I guess I encouraged it, to some extent. I always left a meal for him. He never had to go to a store and buy something, or figure out certain things, because I took care of them. He never would have taken an apartment in New York and been away from me for all the nights Dan is away."

Here she was referring to my husband and the small apartment we bought together in New York a few years ago, when he needed to be there more for work. Sometimes I go with him—I have work and friends and colleagues there—and sometimes I stay at our Massachusetts home with our dogs. This is a living arrangement we both chose and both love; after almost three decades of being a mother and wife myself, I have back the solitude I crave, along with a loving family. But I think it's interesting that my mother sees it as *Dan taking* an apartment, and being *away from* me—as if the choices were all his. I decided to not try to explain this.

"How about," I said, "when he yells at us, or talks over you on the phone? How do you feel about that?"

"He's very nasty about the phone," she admitted. "But he thinks that anything I do with the children, he should be part of. I don't agree, especially because we have three daughters, and I'm their mother, and I think I should be able to talk to them without him listening, but—it's not worth the fight. If I mention to him some detail you told me on email, he'll say, 'How do you know that?' He'll say, 'Why are you emailing Cathi separately? Why do you keep things secret?' He doesn't like anything kept from him."

I nodded; no big news. But she had admitted it's "not worth" fighting him to have access to her daughters—or anyone else;

that, point blank, she chooses placating him over talking to us. I knew that, of course. But it helped to hear her say it now, officially.

"And when he decides what all your trips will be, or what movies you'll see," I said, "are you relieved, on some level? Is it better for you not to have to make all those choices?"

"I'd just rather not fight with him," she said again. "He's difficult, and it's a challenge to always have to comply with his decisions, but it's much easier to comply than to fight. To me, those things really don't make much difference."

I thought of her family then, especially her father: a small, warm, gentle man, round face, light-brown hair all his life. Close to my mother, her two brothers, and all his grandchildren. I remember, when we slept there, waking him at five or six in the morning to watch cartoons with my sister and me, something we weren't allowed to do at home. He was always game. Unlike my father's parents, my mother's parents, Mac and Sylvia, never got angry—at us, or, that I saw, at anyone. Once, when I had an itchy mosquito bite, Mac told me I should try not to scratch it, that I should simply accept that it would itch. I found that mind-boggling. He was trained as a lawyer, but when his father died, instead of getting to practice, he and his brothers took over the family dry-goods store, which employed all three of their families for a long time.

"Do you remember your first fight with him?" I asked my mother.

"No."

"Do you remember when he sent you to drag me out of that high school sports competition, in front of everyone, because he was furious I wasn't home when he got home for dinner? Did that bother you at all?"

"I don't remember that, but I'm sure I was upset." I pictured her walking around as she talked to me, wiping the kitchen counter, straightening the endless piles of newspapers and magazines my father insists on keeping. "There was no question he was the rule maker and the decision-maker, the disciplinarian and the provider," she said. "But I took on all the things I did as being what I was *supposed* to do, and I didn't question it. I felt I didn't have a choice."

"Maybe," I suggested, "in some ways it was a relief to have him do the disciplining of us?"

"Well, I just thought he knew how it had to be. I deferred to him. I didn't always agree with the way he disciplined you—I always thought he was too harsh, too angry sounding. And I did tell him, but he'd say, 'Oh, I wasn't really angry about that.' And I'd say, 'But you *sound* angry, and that's how people perceive you, so—that's a problem for you.'"

She paused. "But you know, Cathi, he also was very involved in the athletic pursuits of all of you children." This is true. When I was young, he threw the baseball with me, and, later, with my brother. He played tennis with me almost as much as I asked, which was a lot. He taught me to be tough. "And he's extraordinarily nice to—" She mentioned a close friend of theirs whose husband had recently died. "He picked her up and took her

27

to dinner with us last weekend and then drove her home, and she really appreciated that. He's very loyal to old friends."

Again, fair enough. "How about when he fought with the tour guide at that national park?" I asked.

"I was really mad," she said. "I felt trapped and humiliated and angry. And I did say something to him about it, but he didn't see it my way at all—and he still doesn't. To this day. A friend recently went on that trip and he was talking to her about it and describing that tour. He agrees he was obnoxious, but he feels the tour guide deserved it, that he wasn't getting out of the trip what he'd paid for, so he had a right to complain. I felt— I mean, he said 'Fuck you' to her [the guide]. I don't really think that's the way to ingratiate yourself with fellow travelers." She paused. "But honestly, I don't remember all these little things! Not until they're brought up again. And I *do* think it's a healthy denial that allows my marriage to continue."

I nodded. I have noticed that in many, if not all, longtime marriages, there's both pragmatism and some (healthy?) denial. "And how about when P [my daughter] left college freshman year?" I said. "Do you remember the way he reacted?" I refreshed her memory. Dismissing the opinion of P's therapists both at home and at school, who agreed she should take time before being there, he wrote irate, condemning emails to both her and me, calling her a spoiled brat and demanding I force her to stay. "Are you gonna let her control you forever?" he yelled at me, and to her: "Will you ever let your brother have his turn for attention?" As if taking a leave from college was a ploy by her to be the queen of our house—just as he was king of his.

"I think he thinks you should discipline your kids more sometimes," was my mother's answer, "the way *he* did *you*. He didn't support you when you let her leave college, but he's very happy with the result." Of course he is. After a year of working and figuring out some things, my daughter returned to school and excelled, graduating recently—one year late—with friends, accolades, and job experience she wouldn't have had if she hadn't taken that year. My father came to her graduation, beaming. All was as it should have been again.

"And you?" I asked my mother. "How did *you* feel at that time?"

"I was worried about her," she said, "and it seemed you thought it necessary for her to take time off, so I thought— I mean, she's your child. I thought whatever you thought the best way to deal with it was what we should support. I'm sure I told him that." I remember her staying utterly silent on the topic, though who knows what she said behind the scenes?

I asked her about my youngest sister, Amy, a successful executive who started and runs a think tank of thirteen, and with whom my father also fights—for a while now, I think, more than with me.

"He's very proud of Amy and her work," my mother said. "He thinks she's very smart." I laughed. Smarter than I am, of course, as her SAT scores were higher and she went to Cornell. "And he thinks she's a good mother and wife," she added. "I think he's sorry when he has episodes with Amy." She paused. "And with everyone! But he doesn't want to take the blame."

This is true. My father almost never apologizes. The only thing I've heard him express real remorse for is "letting" my brother move to San Diego for graduate school in his twenties, because San Diego is where his accident happened. If only he'd been close to home, the thinking likely goes, my father could have watched over him better.

Well, listen. I cannot imagine losing a child, cannot imagine how anyone goes on. He can think whatever he wants about that. While I was contemplating all this, my mother said, "But you know, Cathi, you want to take on everything with him. And I think it's better to let some things go. It's like you're always looking to correct him, or—you're *on* him. Amy gets louder and more aggressive at times, but she also engages with him a lot about political things and other things, so they have a deep connection. With you, it's just more antagonistic."

Once more, fair—and helpful, in some ways. As the firstborn and the sister arguably most affected, back then, by his narcissism and authoritarianism, I don't cut him much slack.

"When he goes on Facebook as you," I said, "does that ever bug you?" He doesn't have his own Facebook page, so he uses hers. There he comments on the threads of her "friends"—me, for example—sometimes with attempted humor, sometimes antagonism, for my own friends and readers (many of whom I don't know) to see. I sign on and shake my head. Delete delete delete.

"He doesn't go on as me," she said. "He always signs his initials." Never mind that it's her face and her name, or that sometimes he forgets the initials, or that few, if any, of those who see his comments understand that "LBH not BFH" at the end of the post means it's him, not her. Once, I told her if she didn't control him, I'd have to unfriend her. It worked for about a week.

I said, finally, "Were you ever scared of him? Did you ever have a fight where you felt like leaving?"

"I think a few times," she said, as if she can't quite recall. "It bothers me when he yells. But I never would have left. We have a life together. Whatever it was, it would get straightened out." She paused. "And I don't think he yells so much anymore."

I laughed. If love is blind, love is also, apparently, deaf. My father is the same person he always was—at least for the fifty-five years I've known him. And so is my mother.

I thanked my lovely, sweet mother for her time and her honesty, and we hung up our phones.

So here is the end of my story—the epilogue, maybe. In 1953, my mother met the man of her dreams, and in 1957, they married. In a scoop-neck white dress, barely over nineteen years old, she pledged to have him and hold him, for better and for worse, 'til death did them part. In her diligent green eyes, and as the daughter of a gentle, loving man who believed that you accept what life deals you with a smile and a nod, she entered into a lifelong agreement where my father would provide for her and make the decisions, and she would accept them—and that's what she's done. In exchange, she's gotten a faithful, loyal husband, one who screams and yells and loses his temper and humiliates her now and then, one who at times spanked and berated her children, but one who also provided for her and those children, enriched her life with culture, and relied on her as surely and heavily as she relied on him. Was he abusive, or just inflexible and empathy-challenged? Really, does it matter? A label is only that. And as Elie Wiesel said, the opposite of love is not hate, but indifference—and one thing you could never call my father was indifferent. He was there. Front and center, in your face, all the time. And through six decades, four children, six grandchildren, many dogs, many travels, my mother has been okay with that. She has stood by his side, putting him first.

The mystery of my mother is solved, then, and it's this: There *is* no mystery—and in fact, it's only my desire to make it otherwise that's kept it from being downright banal. Like her own father, my mother deals with life's frustrations and devastations mostly by waiting them out and not analyzing too much; by keeping busy, turning a blind eye if needed, helping the truly disadvantaged when she can, and not letting the shit get her down. Unlike me, she didn't and doesn't *need* answers for all of life's questions; she made her bed at sixteen, and now, sixty-five years later, she still lies in it, sanguine and content. She is exactly what I see, and exactly what she wants to be; what she wants is, most of the time, just what she has, and the rest of the time she endures until things improve. As my father said to me recently when he saw me doing whatever I was doing, trying to open some can of worms, "She's happy. Don't make her think she's not."

He is right. And so I don't anymore. After all, her story is her story: a love story, with her own happy ending.

And my story—about love, yes, but also about forgiveness—is mine.

Thesmophoria

By Melissa Febos

I. Kathodos

Steam seemed to rise from the sidewalks of Rome. It was July of 2015, the air thick with heat, cigarette smoke, and exhaust. I had been awake for almost twenty-four hours, three of which I had spent waiting at the airport for an available rental car. I had driven into the city amid bleating horns and the growl of mopeds that darted like wasps around cars. I parked in a questionable spot and wove through the crowded sidewalks until I found the address of my rental. In the tiny apartment, I pulled the curtains and crawled into the strange bed with its coarse white sheets. I posted a photo on Facebook of my shiny exhausted face—*Italia!*—and fell instantly asleep.

Three hours later, I woke to the ding of my phone. I had

three text messages from my mother. Months previous, she had cleared her schedule of psychotherapy patients and purchased her ticket to Naples, where I would pick her up at the airport in four days. From there, we would drive to the tiny fishing town on the Sorrento Coast where her grandmother had been born, and where I had rented another apartment for a week.

You are in Italy??

My ticket is for next month!

Melly???

A spear of dread pierced through the fog of my jet lag, turning my stomach. Praying that I had not made such a colossal mistake, I frantically scrolled through our emails, scanning for dates. It was true. I had typed the wrong month in our initial correspondence about the trip. Weeks later, we had forwarded each other our ticket confirmations, which obviously neither of us had read closely. My head hummed with anxiety.

The panic I felt was more than my disappointment at the ruin of our shared vacation, to which I had so been looking forward. It was more than the sorrow I felt at what must have been her hours of panic while I slept, or her imminent disappointment. It was more than the fear that she would be angry with me. Who wouldn't be angry with me? My mother's anger never lasted.

Imagine a foundation as delicate and intricate as a honeycomb, a structure that could easily be crushed by the careless hand of error. No, imagine a structure that has weathered many blows, some more careless than others. The dread I felt did not rise from my thoughts but from my gut, from some corporeal logic that had kept meticulous track of every mistake before this one. That believed there was a finite number of times one could break someone's heart before it hardened to you.

For the first year, it was just us two. My mother, who had been such a lonely child, wanted a daughter. Then she had me. It was the first story I understood to be mine. Melissa, which means "honey bee," was the name of the priestesses of Demeter. Melissa, from *meli*, which means "honey," like Melindia or Melinoia, those pseudonyms of Persephone. We all know the story: Hades, king of the underworld, falls in love with Persephone and kidnaps her. Demeter, her mother and the goddess of agriculture, goes mad with grief. During her relentless search for Persephone, the fields go fallow. Persuaded by Demeter and the pleadings of hungry people, Zeus commands Hades to return Persephone. Hades obeys but first convinces Persephone to eat four seeds of a pomegranate, thus condemning her to return to Hades for four months of every year—winter.

I don't know how it feels to create a body with your own. Maybe I never will. I remember, though, how it felt to be a daughter of a daughter, the distance between our bodies first none, then some. She nursed me until I was nearly two years old, already speaking in full sentences. Then, she fed me bananas and kefir, whose tartness I still crave. She sang me to sleep against her freckled chest. She read to me and cooked for me and carried me with her everywhere.

What a gift it was to be so loved. More so, to trust in my own safety. All children are built for this, but not all parents to meet it. She was. Not my first father, so she left him. First, we lived with her mother and then in a house full of women who had decided to live without men. One day on the shore, we found our sea captain strumming a guitar, my real father. From the day they met, he never knew one of us without the other. Today when I see him, the first or second thing he says to me is always, *Ah! Just now, you looked exactly like your mother.*

They both dote on the memory of me as a child. Fat and happy, always talking. *You were so cute*, they say. *We had to watch you. You would have walked off with anyone.*

When he was at sea, it was just us again. After my brother was born, it was me in whom she confided about how much harder it got to be left by him. Her tears smelled like sea mist, cool against my cheek. Like they had doted on me, I doted on my brother, our baby.

After my parents separated, they tried nesting—an arrangement where the children stay in the family home while the parents rotate in and out of it. The first time my father returned from sea and my mother slept in a room she rented across town, I missed her with a force so terrible it made me sick. My longing felt like a disintegration of self, or a distillation of self—everything concentrated into a single panicked obsession. My toys all drained of their pleasure. No story could rescue me. To protect my father, whose heart was also broken, I hid my despair. In secret, I called her on the telephone and whispered, *Please come get me*. I had never been apart from her. I hadn't known that she was my home.

My birthday falls during the fourth month of the ancient Greek calendar, also the month of Persephone's abduction, the month Demeter's despair laid all the earth to waste. During it, the women of Athens celebrated Thesmophoria. The rites of this three-day fertility festival were a secret from men. They included the burying of sacrifices—often the bodies of slain pigs—and the retrieval of the previous year's sacrifices, whose remains were offered on altars to the goddesses and then scattered in the fields with that year's seeds.

When I got my first period at thirteen, my mother wanted to have a party. *Just small, all women*, she said. *I want to celebrate you.* It was already too late. I seethed with something greater than the advent of my own fertility, the hormones catapulting through my body, the fact of our severed family, the end of my child form, or the cataclysm of orgasms I masturbated to each night. These changes weren't all bad. I had been taught by her to honor most of them. But there were things for which she hadn't prepared me, for which she couldn't have. The sum of it all was unspeakable. I would rather have died than celebrate it with her.

It is so painful to be loved sometimes. Intolerable, even. I had to refuse her.

. . .

The psychologists have a lot of explanations for this. The philosophers, too. I have read about separation and differentiation and individuation. It is a most ordinary disruption, they tell us, necessarily painful. Especially for mothers and daughters. The closer the mother and the daughter are, they say, the more violent the daughter's work to free herself. Those explanations offer something, though I am not looking for permission, atomic explanation, or assurance that ours was a normal break. Not only, anyway. I am also interested in a different kind of understanding. For that, I need to retell our story.

I imagine a beloved. A lover with whom I spend twelve years of uninterrupted, undifferentiated intimacy. A love affair in which the burden of responsibility, of care, is solely upon me. I imagine, also, simultaneous responsibilities. In Demeter's case, the earth's fertility, the nourishment of all people, and the cycle of life and death. After twelve years, my beloved rejects me. She does not leave. She does not cease to depend on me—I still must clothe and feed her, ferry her through each day, attend to her health, and occasionally offer her comfort. Mostly, though, she becomes unwilling to accept my tenderness. She exiles me from her interior world almost entirely. She is furious. She is clearly in pain and possibly in danger. Every step I take toward her, she backs farther away.

Of course, this is a flawed analogy. I turn to it because we have so many narratives to make sense of romantic love, sexual love, marriage, but none that feel adequate to the heartbreak my mother must have felt. The only way that I can imagine it is through these known narratives, and the kinds of love I have known. The attachment styles that define our adult relationships are determined in that first relationship, aren't they? I have felt more than a few times the shock of losing access to a lover; it doesn't matter who leaves. It feels like a crime against nature. To continue to live in the presence of that body would be a kind of torture. It must have been, for her. It must have been how Demeter felt as she watched Persephone be carried away in that black chariot, the earth broken open to swallow her.

II. Nesteia

I had spent that Saturday at the library with Tracy. That was what I had told her. When I got in the car that evening, the sun was half-sunk behind the buildings in town. The spring afternoon's warmth had turned cool, a breeze from the nearby harbor bringing the soft clang of a buoy's bell. I slid into the passenger seat, buckled my seat belt, and waved goodbye to Tracy. She turned to walk home. My mother and I watched her retreat, the edge of her T-shirt rippling in the wind. Her back was so straight. She did walk a little bit like a robot, as Josh had observed as he groped in my underwear, breath hot against my neck. My mother's focus shifted onto me.

You smell like sex, Melissa, she said. Her voice wasn't angry or surprised or cruel, only tired. In it was a plea. *Please*, it said, *just tell me the truth. I know it already. Let's be in this together.*

It was easy to present the shock of my humiliation as the shock of incredulity. I had done so before and we both knew it.

I've never had sex, I said. I believed this.

My mother eased into first gear and turned toward the parking lot exit. *Sex isn't just intercourse*, she said. We drove home in silence.

I don't know if we had a conversation about trust that night. We had had them so many times before, my mother trying to broker an understanding, to cast a single line across the distance between us. If trust was broken, my mother explained, it had to be rebuilt. But the sanctity of our trust held no currency with me, so broken trust came to mean the loss of certain freedoms. It didn't work. She didn't want to revoke my freedoms; she wanted me to come home to her. Probably I knew this. If she didn't like the distance my lies created, then she would like even less my silence and sulks, my slammed bedroom door. Of course I won. We each had something the other wanted, but I alone had conviction.

How many times could she call me a liar, or believe me one? I was relentless in my refusal to acknowledge what we both knew. I slept over at friends' homes where older brothers coaxed me into closets or found me in the kitchen at midnight with a glass of water. I went on drug deliveries with a friend's mother who dealt them. I snuck boys into our home or met them behind the movies. Grown men groped me in backyards and basements, on docks and in doorways, and there was nothing she could do.

• • •

The Rape of Persephone is depicted by hundreds of artists, across hundreds of years. The word *rape* translates as a synonym for *abduction*. In most of them, Persephone writhes in the arms of Hades, torquing her soft body away from his muscled arms, his enormous bulging thighs. In Gian Lorenzo Bernini's famous baroque sculpture, Hades's fingers press into her thighs and waist, the white stone yielding so fleshlike. Her hands often push against his face and head, a motion that evokes the response of an actual rape victim. Some of these works resemble that other violation more than others. In Rembrandt's *Rape of Proserpine*, as his chariot plunges through foaming water into darkness and the Oceanids cling to her satin skirts, Hades grasps Persephone's leg around his pelvis, though her gown hides the rest.

My mother surely feared that I would be raped. It was a legitimate danger. In hindsight, I am surprised that it never happened. Perhaps because I feared it as much as she did. Or because I so often yielded to those who would have forced me.

It must have felt like an abduction to her, as if someone had stolen her daughter and replaced her with a maenad. I chose to leave her, to lie, to chase those places where men with muscled thighs might lay their hands on me, but I was still a child. Who, then, was my abductor? Can we call him Hades, the desire that filled me like smoke, that chased everything else out? I was frightened, yes, but I followed him. Perhaps that was the scariest part.

A convention of Spartan weddings widely adopted across Greece was for a groom to seize his writhing bride across his body and "abduct" her by chariot, in a seemingly perfect simulacrum of Persephone's abduction.

We all know the allure of the reluctant lover. But what of our own heart's division? My ambivalence tormented and compelled me. That eros an engine that hummed in me, propelled me away from our home into the darkness. I knew it was dangerous. I couldn't tell the difference between my fear and desire—both thrilled my body, itself already a stranger. And daughters were supposed to leave their mothers, to grope through the dark for the bulging shapes of men, and then resist them. My mother must have anticipated this, must have hoped she would be spared.

But wasn't my mother also my beloved, my captor? Wasn't it against her arms that I fought most viciously? Like the Spartan bride, my heart would have broken if she had truly let me go. A daughter is wedded to her mother first.

In the Homeric *Hymn to Demeter*, the author tells that "for nine days did the Lady Demeter / wander all over the earth, holding torches ablaze in her hands." After that, she takes a human form and becomes the caretaker of an Eleusinian boy, whom she tries and fails to make immortal.

My mother became a psychotherapist. She took a woman lover with long blond hair who loved us while our mother rode a Greyhound bus to the city and back with a word processor propped on her lap. The job of a therapist is to understand ex-

actly these sorts of things. The job of a therapist is not so different from that of a mother, though it is safer. It is collaboration
and it is care, but it is not symbiosis. It is not reciprocal in its
need. Her patients may have been the Eleusinian children who
could never be made immortal, but she helped them as I would
not be helped.

When I told her, just a few months short of seventeen, that I
was moving out, she didn't try to stop me. I knew that she didn't
want me to go. *Maybe I should have tried to stop you*, she has said
to me since, more than once. *But I was afraid that I would lose you
for good.*

I try to remember. I knew that tension between us, how it
could have snapped. By the time I moved out, I had already soft-
ened some. If she had objected, would I have left? No, I think,
though maybe that is the wish of my adult self for that girl. Either way, I would have found the underworlds that followed.

Hades had agreed to return Persephone to her mother. Zeus insisted and he capitulated, on one condition: if Persephone had
tasted any food of the underworld, she would be consigned to
return to Hades for half of every year. Did Persephone know?
Yes and no. In some versions, she thinks she is smart enough to
evade him, to taste and still go home. There are so many holes
in myths, so many iterations and mutations, most unstamped by
chronology. A myth is the memory of a story passed through
time. Like any memory, it changes. Sometimes by will, or neces-
sity, or forgetting, or even for aesthetic purpose.

The pomegranate seeds were so lovely, like rubies, and so sweet. In every version of the story, she tastes them.

I didn't start with heroin. I started with meth, though we called it crystal, which sounded much prettier than the burnt clumps of tinfoil that littered our apartment or the singed smell in the air, as if an oven had been left on too long.

Imagine Persephone's first season in hell. The phone calls home. *I'm sorry I haven't called. I've been busy with classes. I'm making such nice friends.*

My lies were half-true. I was in classes. I did make friends. I had a job and homework and a mattress in the pantry soaked in cat urine that only cost $150 per month. My mother would have paid for more. With it, she would have also bought more claim on the truth.

When I rode that same Greyhound bus home and ate her warm food and stared over the land of my childhood, lush with life, it *was* like rising from some underworld to the golden light of earth. I missed it so much. I couldn't wait to leave. That itch in me like desire, like hunger, like certain kinds of love.

Imagine Persephone loving him. Is it so impossible? We often love the things that abduct us. We often fear the ones we love. I imagine I would find a way, if I were bound to someone for half of the rest of my life. No, for half of eternity. She was immortal. Besides, she could not even have escaped him by dying.

It was Christmas or Thanksgiving. My mother, my brother, and I joined hands around the table, the steaming food encircled by our arms. We squeezed each other's fingers, pressed our thumbs into each other's palms. That small triad, who had been so sad and so strong in my father's absence. Who had loved each other so fiercely and still did.

After the dishes were washed, my mother sank into the sofa and smiled at us. She was so happy that I was home.

Should we play a game? Watch a movie?

I need to borrow your car, I said.

I can hardly bear to remember her face. As if I'd crumpled her heart and tossed it away.

Where could you possibly have to go tonight?

I don't remember what I answered, only that she let me and how much it hurt to leave them. I pulled the front door shut behind me and something tore inside, like a cloth that still hasn't mended. Still, the quickening as I lit a cigarette in the dark and turned off of our road toward the highway. I imagine that this is the way a man feels leaving his family for his mistress. I did feel part father, part husband. Maybe every daughter does. Or just the ones whose fathers have gone.

I didn't tell her when I stopped shooting up, stopped everything. She had never known that I started. She knew what she saw and that was bad enough. You can't crawl up to your mother from hell and not look like it. If I told her why she didn't have to worry anymore, I'd have to tell her why she worried. I'd have to be done for good. What if Persephone had told Demeter not only what happened in hell, but that she *might* be coming home for good?

What daughter would do that? Besides, there was so much more to Hades than heroin.

A year into my job as a dominatrix, my mother came to visit me in New York. She knew about my job. It was a sexless feminist pursuit. Activism, really. Or, acting, at least. Like so many times before, she didn't challenge me.

One evening as we were leaving to go to dinner, she spotted a harness and dildo hanging from the back of my bedroom door. I don't think I wanted her to see it; I really was that careless.

I know what they make you do with that, she said, her voice brave. I said nothing. To avoid the pain of it now, I think how easily it might have been for my own personal use just a few years later. That would have been embarrassing, but far less painful. But it wasn't a few years later and it hadn't been for my own personal use. Did she know what they "made" me do with it? Probably. I won't imagine how she learned that.

It wasn't that we didn't talk about sex. We sometimes did. What we didn't talk about were the things I designated. The parts of me she might find illegible. The things she might have disapproved of, or simply been hurt by, or that I had no words to name.

He's not so bad, Mother, Persephone could have said. *It's hard to explain. It's a whole other world down here. It's half my home.* Though I can understand why she wouldn't.

Another holiday. After dinner, all of us draped over the couch, drowsy with food.

I need to borrow your car, I said.

Her pleading face, so pretty and so sad.

Where could you possibly be going?

I took a breath.

I have to go to a meeting, I said. Then I had to explain. *It was bad,* I said.

She wanted to know how bad or thought she did.

Bad, I said.

I told her very little and it still hurt a lot.

It all makes so much more sense now, she said. Her face was so tired. I wanted to take it all back.

How much are you supposed to tell someone who loves you that much, whom you want to protect? Is it worse for them to find out later, when you are safe on the other side? I hated to watch my mother sort through the past, solving the puzzle of my inconsistencies with the pieces I'd withheld. Lies make fools of the people we love. It's a careful equation, protecting them at the cost of your betrayal. Like mortgaging the house again to pay for the car. I was also, always, protecting myself. There were things I would no longer be able to believe if I had to say them aloud. I could only tell her the truth when I faced it.

Three years later, I sent her the book I'd written.

You can't call me until you've finished reading it, I said. In it were all the things I'd never told her about the heroin and the parts of that job that hadn't felt like feminist activism or even acting. *Take as much time as you need*, I said, hoping that she would take as much time as she needed to not need to talk to me about how it felt to read those things.

She agreed.

The phone rang the next morning at 7 a.m.

Mom? You were supposed to wait until you finished reading the book to call me.

I did.

You did?

I couldn't stop. I kept putting it down and turning out the light and then turning it back on and picking it back up again.

Why?

I had to know that you were going to be all right.

It was the hardest thing she'd ever had to read, she said. It was a masterpiece, she said.

In the years that followed, she sometimes told me about the awkward things her colleagues would say to her about the book, the ways she had to explain my past and the ways that she couldn't.

I've had my own experience of it, she once said. I knew she meant that she wanted me to make room for how it had been hard for her, too. The living and the telling. I had made a choice to tell the world the things I couldn't talk about. In doing so, I had forced myself to talk about them, though I still barely could with her. My choice revealed those things to her and simultaneously

forced her to have a conversation with the world. Even more unfair, I didn't want to know about it. I couldn't even bear to listen.

Ten years later, I had a lover who lavished me with gifts and
grand gestures of affection. She wanted me to always be focused on her. When I was, she rewarded me. When I wasn't,
she punished me, mostly by withdrawing. When she withdrew,
I felt a touch of that old disintegration, that sickened longing.
It was torment. It was a compelling cycle and one that I con-
sented to.

The first time I brought this lover home, she wouldn't look
at my mother. She only looked at me. At dinner, she answered
questions but did not ask them. Her eyes sought mine as if tending something there. It was hard for me to look anywhere else.

She's so focused on you, my mother said. *It's odd.*

My lover had brought a gift for my mother, a necklace made
of lavender beads, smooth as the inside of a mussel shell. In
the bedroom, she removed the small box from her suitcase and
handed it to me.

Give it to her, she said.

But it's from you, I said.

It's better if you give it to her, she said.

I knew that my mother would also find this odd. As odd as the
way she only looked at me. As odd as the way my lover needed to
be alone with me for so much of such a short visit.

We'll give it to her together, I said.

It was tempting in the months after I left her to interpret this behavior as an expression of my lover's guilty conscience. But I don't think she knew enough about herself to feel guilty in front of my mother. More likely, she saw my mother as a competitor. I suspect that she feared my mother would see something in her that I couldn't yet. My mother did anyway. Still, I loved that woman for two years. Two years during which I withdrew from my mother almost entirely. I could not see what was happening to me and didn't want to. Like my lover, I refused to look at my mother. I didn't want to see what she saw.

A few times, I called her, sobbing. I had done this when I was on heroin, also.

Do you think I am a good person? I asked.

Of course, she said. I could feel how much she still wanted to help me. I hung up the phone. I missed her so much, worse than ever before.

The morning that I finally decided to leave that lover, I called my mother. This time, I did not wait three years to write a book about it and then send it to her.

I am leaving her, I said. *It's been so much worse than I told you.*

How worse? she asked me, and I told her. *Why didn't you tell me?* she asked.

I don't know, I said. I was weeping. *What if I had told you and then didn't leave her?*

She was quiet for a moment. *Did you think that I would hold that against you?*

I wept harder and covered my eyes with my hand.

Listen to me, she said, her voice strong and unwavering as a hand under my chin. *You could never lose me. I will love you every day of your life. There is nothing you could do to make me stop loving you.*

I didn't answer.

Do you hear me?

III. Kalligeneia

When I sent my second book to my mother, we had an hours-long conversation. I explained how my writing created a place where I could look at and talk to parts of myself that I otherwise couldn't. She explained to me that this was exactly what her mode of therapy allowed her patients to do. We had talked about this before, but never in so much depth.

A few months later, we stood in front of a room packed with therapists, at a conference my mother attends every year. She began the workshop by leading them through an explanation of the clinical model that she primarily uses in her practice and travels around the world training other clinicians in. It was impossible not to watch her. She was warm and funny and expert and charismatic. You could easily see why our mailbox filled with heartfelt cards from patients she'd stopped seeing decades ago. When she was done, I stood. I spoke for a while about how writing allows me to retread the most painful parts of the past and find new meaning there, find healing there. Then, I led them all through a writing exercise that exemplified this and drew upon my mother's therapy model. The therapists scribbled in their notebooks and then I invited a few to share their work. As they read, the group nodded and laughed. A few people wept.

That whole weekend, people clasped our hands and praised our work together. They marveled at the miracle of our collaboration. *How special*, they said. *Whose idea was this?*

Hers, I told them.

There is an older version of Demeter's story. As the memories of stories are changed with each telling, they are more irrevocably changed with each conquer, each colonizer, each assimilation of one people into another. This one existed before the Greek or Roman versions that we know so well and is believed to have emerged from a system of matrifocal mythology, and likely a society whose values it reflected.

There was no rape, no abduction. The mother, goddess of the cycle of life and death, passed freely from the underworld to earth, receiving those who died as they passed from one to the next. Her daughter, some versions say, was simply the maiden version of that goddess, imbued with the same powers. Others suggest that Phesephatta was the very old goddess of the underworld, and always had been.

It used to scare me that I wanted things my mother wouldn't understand. I think we both feared our difference. In hiding it from her, I often created exactly the thing I wished to avoid. It's not that I should have told her everything—that would have been its own kind of cruelty. Though I could have trusted her more. That younger version of our story, the one I have carried for most of my life, the one I have mostly told here, is also true: I hurt myself and I hurt her over and over. But like the old myth, there is another version, a wiser one.

It's not that Persephone ever gets to come home. She is already home. The story is used to explain the cycle of seasons, of life. Her time spent in the dark is not an aberration of nature, but its enactment. I've come to see mine the same way. Like Persephone, my darkness has become my work on this earth. I return to my mother again and again, and both realms are my home. There is no Hades, the abductor. There is only me. There is nothing down there that I haven't found a piece of in myself. I am glad to have learned that I do not have to hide this from her. It helps that the darkness is less likely now than ever to kill me.

I can hold both of these stories. There is room for one in the other. First, the sacrifice made on the first day of Thesmophoria, Kathodos, a ritual violence. The other, retrieved on the third day, Kalligeneia, and sprinkled in the fields. The sacrifice becomes the harvest. All of my violences might be seen this way: a descent, a rise, a sowing. If we sow them, every sacrifice can become a harvest.

As the Rome traffic heaved outside the window of that tiny apartment, I stared at my phone, that dread thickening in me. I understood that I could sink this whole trip into it, spend every day punishing myself for my mistake. I didn't have to, though. The part of me who feared our bond too fragile to withstand this blow was a young part. I had to tell her about this new story. I had to tell her that there was nothing I could do that would make my mother stop loving me. I promised her. Then, I called my mother.

She was mad, of course, and disappointed, but by the end of the call we were laughing.

A few days later, I phoned her from the town where her grandmother was born.

You are going to love it here, I said.

There is a difference between the fear of upsetting someone who loves you and the danger of losing them. For a long time, I couldn't separate them. It has taken me some work to discern the difference between the pain of hurting those I love and my fear of what I might lose. Hurting those we love is survivable. It is inevitable. I wish that I could have done less of it. But no matter how much of it I did, I would never have lost her.

A year later, I picked her up at the Naples airport, and we drove down the coast to that town. For two weeks, we ate fresh tomatoes and mozzarella, and walked the streets that her grandmother had walked. I drove us all the way down the Amalfi Coast Highway and only scratched the rental car a little bit.

As I drove, my mother held my phone up to film the shocking blue waters that rippled below, the sheer drop from the highway's edge, the wheeling birds that seemed to follow us, and the tiny villages built into the hillside. It was terrifying and beautiful, like all my favorite journeys.

Back home, I sorted through the pictures, deleting the doubles and smiling at our happy faces. When I got to that video and played it, I saw an image of her sandaled foot—wide and strong like my own—on the gritty floor of the rented Fiat. Our voices, recorded with perfect clarity, commented on the scenery. I realized that she had been holding the phone's camera upside down the whole time. I snorted and kept watching her shifting foot as we remarked on a passing bus. Then, I closed my eyes and listened to our conversation moving eagerly from subject to subject, our gasps as mopeds sped by us on hairpin turns, and our laughter ringing on and on.

Xanadu

By Alexander Chee

We were allowed to testify in a room by ourselves, taped testimony, because we were minors. As I sat in the waiting room with one of the other boys, a friend of mine, he said, with a shrug, "I let him give me a blow job." He leaned back after he said it, and then held out his hands. "I mean, I'm okay. It didn't hurt me."

I nodded and wondered if I felt the same way.

We were fifteen, almost sixteen. We had been in the same boys choir for years and had both just left, our voices having changed. I had seen the boys from the choir have to change schools once the details came out in the press. I already knew that people treated us, the victims, as if we were also criminals. I had discovered the way everyone has an opinion when they discover you were sexually abused. Everyone seems to think immediately of how they'd have handled it better, and they expect you to answer their questions to confirm this. To come forward, especially if you're a boy, is to be told you failed, implicitly, or even explicitly.

I had agreed to testify but had not identified myself as a victim. The director faced fifteen counts.

I tried out my friend's tone. Even his statement.

It wasn't that bad. I knew I was lying to myself, and he was too. I wasn't going to say this lie, not yet. But I could leave myself out.

I would think of this a year later when I had to convince this friend not to kill himself by telling him he wasn't gay.

I can tell you he was my friend, but there isn't really language, a single word, for what and who we were to each other. We were also having a sexual relationship at the time we were about to testify. One that had begun in front of the director, on a camping trip, done to amuse him. Months after that, the relationship began, as if we needed the time to pass. We played Dungeons and Dragons together—he was always the Paladin; I was always a Magic-User. I wasn't in love with him, but I loved him—I still do. I didn't know how to call what we had found a name. Sometimes I've referred to him as my first boyfriend, but we didn't hold hands, didn't go to prom together as dates—when we did go, we were both with girls. What we had begun one day without any words felt more real to me in those moments. We never called it anything. One or the other of us would make a plan to hang out, and it could mean anything. I wonder sometimes if we were consoling each other, but I don't know because we almost never spoke to each other about what we did. His waiting-room admission to me about what had happened that day didn't shock me; I had seen what he was talking about, in front of me.

At the time it had happened, my friends and I in the choir had the habit of drawing elaborate forts, full of soldiers, weapons, planes, submarines—an impossible structure. The choir was like this, it seems to me now. Or I was. Full of secrets too complicated to explain. But maybe a map could say it all. This is an attempt at one.

I had joined the choir at age eleven. The director's approaches to me began at age twelve and had been pitched at both my pride in myself, as a precocious child, and my shame in myself as biracial, queer, a social pariah at my school. He fed my belief that I was talented, intellectually more mature than my peers, and emotionally more mature also, from the beginning. He praised my voice and sight-reading ability at my audition and chose me as a section leader, and then as a soloist. This meant rehearsals alone with him. I trusted him because he made me feel good, even superior, at a time when I felt abandoned by the world. And when I say this, I mean specifically that I was a Korean American biracial child in a town that didn't seem to believe people of different ethnicities would even marry, much less have a child. On any given day I felt like a freak, too visible in the wrong way, which is the same as not being seen.

I had a three-octave voice as a soprano, with forceful top notes, and the ability also to blend that voice with those around me. As a sight reader, able to read the music and sing it decently through the first time around, I was valuable to the learning of the music, and soon I discovered that whatever racism afflicted my class-mates, here I was welcomed as a leader. I became popular and won the affection of friends. At middle school, I was still cornered or excluded. But now at choir, friends surrounded me. I needed a place to belong more than I even knew then. But the director knew. And so he had acted to me as if only he could provide it. This is what I now know is called *grooming the victim.* This choir full of talented boys, many of them outcasts like me, many of them queer, was for a short time my paradise, because it was also a trap, for all of us. Made out of us.

On the surface it looked as if I was going to choir practice, but inside, each day I went, I was running away from home. To what felt like the only place in the world that would accept me and nurture me. As we sang for larger and larger audiences, their applause felt like a relief I could never have imagined.

The director's crimes were revealed the same year we mourned my father, who died on a January day almost three years to the day after his accident—a period that was almost the entire time I was in the choir. At the time I speak of, I was my mother's right hand and had become so immediately. The day the phone call came from the hospital telling us my father had been in a car accident, she left to be at his side, leaving us behind in the house with a family friend until more was known. I don't remember that I was able to do anything but remain in the family room, across from the phone, waiting for her to call. In those first moments, between when the family friend taking care of us arrived and my mother left, I knew this was the moment my father had spoken of when he told me that if anything ever happened to him, I was to be the man in the family, and something in me changed accordingly.

When she called and the phone rang, it shot up into the air and flew toward me as if I had lifted it with my mind. The telekinesis I had longed for while reading comics, suddenly there, as if released by the crisis, just like in those stories. But if it was, I apparently locked it up right away. This never happened again.

When I picked the receiver up, it was my mother, speaking to me, barely able to say what she was saying, and I knew we were in a new world.

My father had been in a head-on collision, and his business partner, the driver, less seriously injured, died a few days later. My father was in a coma for three months. We went to the hospital to read to him in turns, our voices said to help him return to consciousness. I don't recall the book, just the reversal, the man who used to tell me stories, now apparently listening to me from within this coma, as if I could guide him with one. What I could tell no one now as I sat by his bed, reading to him, was as huge as my life: I blamed myself for my father's accident.

The previous fall, I had asked for permission to skip swim

practice so I could go on a roller-skating trip with the Webelos. I was not an experienced skater but my favorite movie in the world then was *Xanadu*, and I wanted to skate around the rink and imagine myself singing along to the songs, covered in light like Olivia Newton-John—and secretly imagining I was her. But instead I fell off my skates that night and landed on my left arm. When I looked at it, it was crooked, like a branch on a tree. I let out a scream perhaps only a boy soprano could, one that stopped the music in the rink, and in my memory there is a spotlight on my arm, before I began my scream, at which point the other skaters stopped to look on in horror as the disco stops.

My mother, on her way to the rink, pulled over to let the ambulance pass by, wondering who had been hurt.

At the hospital, I recall the doctor setting my arm, saying the device he was inserting my fingers into was like a medieval torture device, something made for interrogations, now used to help separate the broken bones so they could be set properly. The old torture machine pulled my arm smooth. The arm was x-rayed, wrapped in a cast. Soon I was home, contrite, logy with pain medication. Over the next few days I learned that as I could no longer go to swim practice, my coach was furious. And we would not be going to Florida on vacation, as I would just get sand in my cast.

The night of my father's accident, when his car slid in the snow and ran into the car in the other lane, I told myself we were to have been safely on a beach, and I never forgot it. I waited to be blamed. The cast was still on my arm, itchy and strange. But no one said anything to me.

Thirty-five years would go by before I would tell my mother this. I had finally realized my theory about it was a memory but one I wasn't sure I should trust. The shock on her face was terrible to see, like she was watching me turn into something she never knew could exist. "We had to cancel the trip because of your father's work," she said. "Not because of your arm. We would never have done that." I tried to see if I believed her. I knew at least she believed herself.

Had I made up the conversation I was sure I remembered, telling me the trip was off? It made sense that my arm alone wouldn't have stopped us—it was an international, multimillion-dollar deal my father was working on, after all. He wouldn't take a family vacation in the middle of it. This was the deal my father believed was his ship coming in. He had been taking me to see luxury cars, as he was going to buy one to treat himself. Or he drove them to us, picking us up at school for a test drive. One week he came to school in a Mercedes convertible, white with red leather interior. The next day, an Alfa Romeo. The next day, a Jaguar. He was so full of joy as he pushed the door open, his smile so bright. And then came that winter.

Years later classmates confessed they had thought we were rich, and all the cars were ours.

With distance I can see how, as unbearable as his injuries were to him—paralyzed down the left side of his body, the accident had drawn a rough line down his center—all his dreams were broken too. He'd been a martial artist since childhood, and his conditioning was such that he had survived this crash that had taken the life of the driver, less severely injured. He had trained his whole life to survive no matter what, and now he had, and he wanted to die.

He had been so strong all my life, this man who raced me in holding my breath underwater just months before, doing fifty, seventy-five yards without a breath. The man who had taken me into the basement to teach me to box, who made me study karate and tae kwon do after the kids at school had cornered me. The man who had thrown me into a wave for crying with fear at the ocean, and then taught me over the years to beat the riptide. "You need to be able to swim well enough that if the boat is going down, you can swim to shore," he told us.

I did not know where the shore for this was.

I am twelve. My hero is my father and he is broken. And I believe I broke him, my own broken arm pushing him into the car. I believed it until four years ago.

Over the three years my father was convalescing from the injuries he would eventually die from, in the first year, after he woke from his coma, he lived at home, in a makeshift bedroom that was once our living room. He was angry and depressed, suicidal at times, and when I got home from school I would visit with him before attending to homework. A cousin from Korea was sent by our family there to live with us, to be his companion, an older man I liked all right, though he seemed fidgety. He watched K-dramas or played cards with my father, who had once been an excellent poker player, and dispelled some of the airless gloom of my father's sadness and fury. We had fought for him to live and he did not want to live now, and it was hard not to feel we'd failed him. My mother taught me how to make several hamburger casseroles—American chop suey, which was really just elbow pasta in a tomato gravy; "Texas hash," which was essentially the same but with rice; and a beef Stroganoff that was made by pouring sour cream and cream-of-mushroom soup onto ground beef, and which I often served on rice also. My mother now worked at the fisheries business; the deal he'd been working on fell apart without the men who had been at its center. She faced the difficulties of being a woman in a business dominated by men, and would come home at the end of the day, exhausted, to the man she had loved enough to marry and defy her family and culture. The stories she told, of the way her work alienated her from many of the women who had been her friends, of the way the men who worked with my father were being won over by her but had to be won over, came out at these times. I would listen, sometimes give her a back rub or a shoulder rub as she confided in me, and bring her a glass of scotch on the rocks. I was, am, a receptive ear, to many, and I learned it here.

I just never knew how to tell her what was happening when I was away from home.

I am known for speaking when everyone else is silent, of saying the thing everyone is thinking but no one will say. And so it is all the stranger to me that I won't say this, won't speak up about this, when I look back, until I remember, for me, it was like a secret paradise. The only pleasure I had besides food was singing. Until it was just another hell. A less terrible one.

A year passes, and my father's sister convinces us she will care for him in her home. A doctor near her in Massachusetts has, she insists, the possibility of restoring him. We take the second cousin and my father there, and for a year, go back and forth to see him. A year after that, when we understand the doctor is really just experimenting on my father, and endangering him, we bring him back to Maine, this time to a facility near us in Falmouth.

The choir becomes bigger, more professional. I had been briefly proud of my leadership and popularity, but once the director had had what he wanted from me, these made me a threat to him. He accuses me of creating cliques with my Dungeons and Dragons games, and tries to isolate me socially. I'm still the section leader, but no more solos. My strange relationship with my friend is now the silent center of my life, the world between us, sex taken when we can find it. The terrible pain of the rest of life is erased in those moments. My memories of him are still another color from the rest, as if they were all lived in another dimension.

A favorite memory of summer is a week at his parents' lake house. We sneak out to the lake at night, and make our way to swim, finding each other eventually in the liquid dark. However we met each other feels erased to me, or worth it somehow, for this. But I don't tell him and so I don't know how he feels.

I wonder sometimes what would have happened if I'd said something there also.

The secrets hidden in me could fill that lake, but don't. They leave with me.

Now I am fifteen. I move through my days like a kind robot, someone whose job is to bring a version of me around to attend to all of the things that need doing. But sometimes there are outbursts, storms of anger. In a fight with my brother, I try to get him to shut up, and when I can't, I get on his chest with my knees. I can still see the startled fear in his eyes.

In my role as the cook, I am near the food, and so I eat. Bagels with cream cheese for breakfast, pepperoni pizza or a hamburger or cheeseburger for lunch, roast beef sandwiches with Muenster cheese, kielbasa and eggs, ham and melted cheddar. Food is our first experience of care, a child psychiatrist tells me, when I go. My mother has sent me because of my eating. I've gained weight. He asks if I feel unloved, and I don't know how to answer that. I eat for the pleasure I feel, the annihilating pleasure of it. I eat because I'm too smart for my own good, too sensitive, too queer, too Asian, too sad, too loud, too quiet, too angry, too fat. I eat because I wanted to go roller-skating, to be surrounded by disco light, and it brought my world down to the ground and I won't ever escape this way, but it feels like I do. As if I could chew my way out of this hell.

When my voice finally changes, it feels like a replacement in my throat, a struggle, like something is dying. The high soprano notes I could sing, the way they illuminated me, my vocal chords like filaments, this all leaves, and it is hard not to feel like a darkness is left behind. It is at least the absence of that specific light. I can hear it still, can still feel the way the notes filled my head and throat like the air I would hold as I went underwater. The vibration of my body to the sounds I could make in my throat was simply a more vigorous way of being alive.

I won't learn to sing with my adult voice for thirty years, when I fall in love with a man who has an adult voice as beautiful as any of the pop stars he covered in his high school band. We will go to karaoke in that distant future, so much so that my own voice will begin to respond as if I am going to rehearsals again. I still don't feel it's the same. It is as if I had a voice that left and another that arrived, and not a voice that changed.

When I give my testimony, that is the voice I use. The newcomer. I describe the trips, the way he would pick a favorite and train him and get him alone by giving him a solo. I don't say I know because he did it to me. I don't say he tried to make me feel special when it seemed like no one else would, or that the room of children, many of them gay, was my first queer community. I don't say that I found my first boyfriend there, and that it let me feel connected to this world when nothing else did, and how so many of us were like that, chosen because we were so much alike—boys who needed someone to prop up our world, who would let him do what he did in exchange for that. Boys without fathers, or with broken ones. Boys with moms who were trying to save their homes. I say it happened to other people; I act like

I'm just being cooperative. I don't say that I wanted to die of the guilt, of feeling that I helped make all of this happen, and that it all happened because I was queer.

This testimony is good practice for when I don't tell about the night my friend called, begging me to tell him he wasn't like me, that he wasn't gay. Telling me he had a shotgun, his dad's, and was ready to kill himself if he was. Tell me, he said. Tell me I'm not like you. And I do. You're not like me, I say. You're not gay. We've spoken of it at last. Because isn't it better to live? For him, at least. I don't say all the times I almost tried, staring at the knife in the kitchen, so often as I made the food, wishing I had the courage to go upstairs, run the bath, and climb in with the blade. Instead I lock all of that up in my throat with everything else. And I leave the courthouse, set to explode years later, like a bomb from an old war, forgotten, until it all surfaces at last.

Twenty years later I stand in my Brooklyn studio apartment and hold my phone in my hand, staring at it with dread. It is the night before my first novel's publication in the fall of 2001, and my mother is about to travel to New York for my launch at the Asian American Writers' Workshop. If I don't make the call, I will read from the novel in front of her, a novel about surviving sexual abuse and pedophilia, inspired by events from my childhood—these autobiographical events, events I have never described for her—and she will find out the next evening in a crowded room full of strangers. And she will never forgive me if I do. So now is the time.

I could tell you I remember the phone call I made, what I said, what she said, but I'd be lying. I call. The borders around this conversation are like something hot was set down on the rest of the memory and it burned. I remember she was shocked, and she didn't understand why I'd never told her. I didn't either, but I do now.

Our family had passed through a season of hell, and this was what I'd done to survive it. I know at last: I never told her about this because I was sure I was protecting her. It wasn't that I was ashamed of it, exactly. I knew it would grieve her. Another disaster. I was her other hand; she needed me. I couldn't be broken too. And so I had hidden myself inside a lesser disaster to survive this one. Hidden myself altogether. My mother, day after day, going to work inside the death of the dream my father had had all those years ago, returning to us—her three children, the man she'd loved, now hurt and wanting to die— she needed me.

The novel I give her the next day details the secrets of the abuse and all that it brought. The story of my father's accident, his despair, his death and how I survived that—that is not in the book, though I tried. "No one will believe this many bad things happened to one person," my first agent had said, and I had cut it from the draft, inventing other apparently more believable destructions. Leaving it out was a way of surviving it all even all these years later. Writing the novel had told me only one of them was bearable, even though I knew I had survived both.

In the audience, as I finish reading from this novel, the world I hid from her now in these sentences, I find my mother's eyes. She is smiling. I can tell it is hard for her but she is proud of me. Prouder than she's ever been.

This is how we got each other through.

16 Minetta Lane

By Dylan Landis

The wives of my father's friends do not iron shirts.

"I'm sure they don't wash floors either," my mother says evenly. She talks to me but also through me. We are alone in the elevator of our New York apartment building, going down to the basement, where a woman named Flossie is going to teach my mother, for two dollars, how to iron a man's shirt.

My mother tells me the wives have degrees in psychology or in social work, and they see patients, like my father does in our living room.

"Let's just say I'm conscious of it," my mother says, and we step out into a vast gray complication of corridors.

It's 1964 and I am eight years old. My public school is so

strict that girls can't wear pants, even in a blizzard. My father is writing his psychology thesis, "Ego Boundaries," which I half believe is the name of some fourth, shadowy person who lives in our apartment. My father teases me that when I grow up, I will get my PhD and take over his practice, and I believe that too.

He doesn't tell my mother that she will get her PhD.

My mother is a housewife.

We walk down a broad hallway with padlocked doors. The super's red-haired daughter, Silda, gets to *live* down here. We roller-skate on the velvety floors and spy on Otto, the porter, who has a number on his arm and sleeps in a storage room behind towers of old newspapers.

The laundry room smells deliciously of wet wool, and it rumbles from the dryers. My mother says hello and how are you to Flossie in a bright voice, and Flossie looks up. She gives my mother the exact same half smile I see her give everyone who talks to her. She has deep folds in her face, and she is dark as a plum and delicate as a bird. Her iron looks heavy. It thumps on the board and the sound is a slow heartbeat that goes on all day.

The wives in our building pay her twenty-five cents a shirt.

I tug wet clothes from our washer. My mother selects a shirt, takes it to Flossie, and hands her money that disappears into a smock the color of clay. Then Flossie wedges the shirt onto the nose of the board.

My father wears a dress shirt every day. If my mother stops giving the shirts to Flossie, we could save five dollars a month.

I pull out rack after screeching metal rack from the wall till I find one that's not full of someone else's clothes hanging stiff and dry over the rods. As I drape my father's socks and undershirts, I watch the lesson: Flossie ironing, then my mother ironing, then my mother listening to Flossie with her head tipped.

She is so beautiful, my mother. She has distant blue eyes and cheekbones like butter knives. Her chin is like one of my grand-mother's porcelain teacups. Once a week she sits for a portrait because an artist in our building, a woman she likes, asked her to model; and I see her slipping out of a cage, those hours, and talking about books and sipping tea with the artist, and watching the Hudson glitter.

Beneath the racks, behind the wall, are gas burners—rows and rows of beautiful orange-blue flames, kept under tight con-trol. Otherwise they would rise up and lick the clothes.

Dryers cost a quarter. The racks are free.

My mother comes over with the shirt on a wire hanger.

"She's an excellent teacher," she says, and calls back to Flossie, "You're an excellent teacher." Then she says, "I've got my work cut out for me."

A few weeks later my father does something startling, right in our living room. He asks my mother to dance.

It's after dinner, and dark out, though for us it's never daylight because our living room and kitchen are on the air shaft, low down, and my bedroom faces a brick wall.

My mother and I clear the table. My father, who usually goes straight to his desk, picks out a record album: *The Boy Friend*.

Records are what we do for fun. We don't have a TV. But we do have this record player made of thick, shiny plastic the color of eggplant. I am not allowed to touch it.

My father lifts the arm over the record and sets the diamond needle down. The overture starts, horns so effusive and cheery I know they're lying. But my parents pretend this is what happiness sounds like.

My father settles on the sofa, unfolding elbows and knees like a praying mantis. My mother opens a book at the other end and tucks her toes under his leg.

"Dance for us, Yum," my father says.

My mother dances?

Ladies start singing now, voices so chipper I want to slap them.

My mother smiles, shakes her head, and keeps reading. The book cover says *The Golden Bowl*. "Come on, Yum," my father says encouragingly. "Dance."

"I'm not a dancer," says my mother.

But she stands.

Julie Andrews sings now that every girl needs a boy friend— that *we would gladly die for him*, which alarms me; it feels fake, like everything else on this record, and also familiar. My mother moves in a new way, at first as if she's testing the air for doneness, and then tangoing her way toward the wall-to-wall bookshelves with a boy friend we cannot see, on a stage that isn't there. She swivels. She bites her lip. "Wow," my father says, but she ignores him. She stalks, points one toe, hikes up her skirt, and pushes her bosom out.

Then the song ends and she sits as if she'd just walked into the room, retucks her toes, and opens *The Golden Bowl* to her bookmark.

"Yum!" my father cries, applauding. "Where'd you learn to do that?"

But he isn't exactly asking, and my mother doesn't exactly answer.

"Oh, I just make it up as I go," she says.

Questions I don't ask my mother that night:

Why don't you dance *every day*?

Why not take your husband's hand and pull him into the dance?

Why not take your daughter's hand and pull her into the dance?

Where does the dancing mother go when she's not here? Where has she been all our lives?

The dancing mother goes into hiding, but three years later, on a spring Saturday, when I am eleven, my father and I blunder into the place where she once lived.

I don't think my mother meant us to see it.

We take the IRT to Fourteenth Street and stroll. My parents love strolling. My father's dream is to stroll in Edinburgh again, and my mother's dream is to stroll in Paris. We go downtown on Sixth Avenue and my parents hold hands. My father sings a song he learned in the navy—Dirty Lil, Dirty Lil lives on top of Garbage Hill. It makes me feel bad. Does he think she wants to live up there, having sailors tease her?

Suddenly women are shouting from high up, and balled-up bits of paper are scattered on the sidewalk like fat, chewed-up pearls, and I want to open one, because they seem to have dropped from a distant world.

"This is not right," my father says grimly.

I always feel I'm dreaming when I walk by the ladies' house of detention. It's tall, with columns of dark windows, and it's a prison, yet ladies are calling out from the inside, and I don't understand what they're shouting. Plus, if they are locked up and out of reach, how can they drop these wadded papers?

What are they trying to *say*?

We walk downtown some more, on narrow streets. Finally I ask, "Why do they drop those paper balls?"

My mother sighs. "They write down their names and phone numbers on those slips," she says. "They're shouting for people to call their husbands and children, and give them messages."

"Like what messages?'" I'm thrilled. These little white balls are like light from stars that died long ago.

"'I love you,'" my mother says brightly. "What else?"

We are deep in the West Village now. My father strolls us into a right turn, back toward Sixth, and my mother stops so abruptly I step on her heel.

If she feels it I can't tell.

We're on the corner of a street with a name you could sing: Minetta Lane, and my mother is looking at the first pink building I have ever seen.

I love it immediately. It is the Barbie DreamHouse I am not allowed to have. The windows have white shutters, and the house has a wrought iron gate. Behind the gate is a little foyer, or passageway, and a black hanging lantern that melts colors onto the walls.

"Oh," my mother says, as if the air just got socked out of her. My father looks at her patiently. He likes to keep moving.

"I used to live here," my mother says. She sounds amazed.

"It's a sweet place, Yum," my father says, and looks at his watch. "Aren't you girls hungry?"

The hunger I feel is so unreasonable I can't parse it, even to myself. But I want to be the daughter of *this* mother, the one who lives in a pink building, the one who dances.

My mother is lost in thought. I watch her. She searches the building with her gaze, looks dreamily through the gate, and then something slips. The muscles around her mouth soften slightly, so that I wonder if she holds her face in a pleasant posture for us much of the time.

It's not a good feeling. I look over at my father, but he is just waiting, amiably watching my mother look at the house, then turning his attention to the Village street scene.

I hold the locked iron gate with both hands and try to will myself inside.

"I scream, you scream," my father says. "We all scream . . ."

"How could you *leave*?" I ask.

My mother touches one of my hands. It stays tight around the iron bar. "The apartment was small and dark," she says gently. "It faced the courtyard. It was nothing special."

But she is wrong. The apartment has sun, and cats, and hanging plants. It has pink walls, like a stage set where the mother can dance. It has a vase of daisies. It has a table set for two.

"I promise you," she says. "The inside was nothing like the outside."

I'm fourteen in 1970 when we live in a suburb of New York called Larchmont. We own a house, barely. My mother still irons my father's shirts. She puts them in the vegetable crisper to keep them wet till she can get to them. She has long since taught me Flossie's art—cuff, cuff, collar, yoke, sleeve, sleeve. We make hospital corners, we mend hems and darn socks and scour rings off tubs. I'm expected to bleach the whites and fold my father's undershorts out of the dryer, which disgusts me, but there is no getting out of it.

My mother's oil portrait now hangs between my bedroom and my parents'. It captures her perfectly—the faraway blue gaze, a sadness so faint it's really not there, bone structure so elegant you want to trace it with a finger. I need to own this painting, and plan to steal it someday.

I'm lounging on the guest bed in my mother's messy study, the room where she types out bills for my father's patients, when she mentions for the first time an artist she once knew. His name was Bill Rivers.

Bill is a man's name. She's only ever talked about my father and, just twice, a man she was married to briefly. All she's said about him was that he killed her darling bulldog, Chiefie, by leaving him in a hot car.

I sit up.

"His name was Haywood, but everyone called him Bill." She peers at my father's handwriting, then releases a clatter from her red Selectric. "This was long before you were born," she says, and swivels in her chair to face me.

"We were just friends," she says. "I didn't understand how good an artist he was, but I knew I liked being with him, and I liked being around the artists he spent time with. Those were some big names. He would take me to a bar in the East Village where painters and writers hung out. And Dylan ... they thought I was *interesting*. I had *wit* in those days."

"Gee," I say. I'm afraid to talk because of the soap bubble shimmering around us.

She sighs. "It was a rapier wit. A group of us would be drinking and talking, painters and sometimes writers, and I was always the one with the line of sarcastic repartee that made everybody laugh."

I'm so riveted I nod, nod, nod till I'm rocking.

"They loved having me there," she says. "And I loved being there with them."

This is not the woman who married my father and raised me.

"Bill and I had pet names for each other," she says. "I called him Country Boy, because he came from a very tiny town in North Carolina."

She begins to rub her legs repetitively through her pants without seeming to realize it. Her palms go ceaselessly up and down her thighs, up and down, up and down.

It's embarrassing. I look at my own hands.

What did he call you? I ask.

"City Girl, of course."

Pet names are a big deal to my mother. She gave my father one. He gave her one. She has a bunch of ridiculous ones for me, like Winning Ways, which sounds like the name of a racehorse to me, and—it's hard to even say aloud—Pussy. So did she go out with this Bill Rivers person?

I'm about to ask another question when my mother swivels back to her desk and draws an explosive burst from the Selectric.

Partly by cheating in French and math, I finish tenth grade. It's early July 1972, the summer of Watergate, and I'm flush, because I've inherited my friend J's part-time job sorting transistors in a TV repair shop. J, who is fifteen, had an affair with the thirty-six-year-old married boss, so I'd been wary, but apparently this was not a requirement.

One day after the shop closes I come home and glimpse my mother locked in grievous conflict with the family checkbook at the dining table. She'll sit like that, arching her back to stretch, for two or three days.

"Dylan, I need you to pick up dinner," she says.

Too late. I've bolted upstairs.

We seem to have more money now. For one thing, she sends the shirts out. For another, last summer my father bought an Alfa Romeo convertible. He doesn't trust me to drive it, and then it gets stolen. This seems like justice to me. Also, we have a gardener every week, which is major, because when we moved here two years ago, guess who mowed and raked.

"I'm going out," I yell down, because I am one of those teenagers now. But the truth is that the sight of her chained to that chair—chaining *herself* to that chair—makes me angry.

It's a monster, this checkbook. My father set it up—a binder whose spreadsheets have the wingspan of a yardstick. Lots of categories run across the top in my mother's tiny, pretty script, and every category needs to be filled in for every check.

I would rather die.

My mother appears in the door of my room. It's painted rose because she rolled up her sleeves and painted it with me, and it's cloudy with cigarette smoke because I don't obey my parents' rules anymore. They don't beat me and they won't throw me out, and you can't yell me into submission.

"I need you to go out for dinner," she says seriously. "Please don't do this now."

By now I'm aware every day that my mother is scarily smart. She got only halfway through college and never says why. But she talks about Turgenev, Shakespeare, Tolstoy, Pritchett, both Eliots, Pound, Lessing, Chekhov, Céline—and she reads books by literary critics. Something inside drives her through books. She says it drove her mother too—Esther, who only got to third grade in Russia before she had to go to work, rolling cigarettes in a factory with other children, bare-fingered in the freezing cold.

I'll never be able to read all those books, I don't want a PhD, and I am doomed to disappoint my intellectual parents. So I do what I'm good at: hanging out with boys, especially boys in their twenties with long hair and cars and drugs.

"I'm late," I say. "And that checkbook is just stupid." And we are off, arguing over a figment we can't even name.

My mother struggles with the numbers on clocks, with left and right, with counting out change at Grand Union. But balancing the checkbook is part of her job. She stays at it, poking the adding machine with the eraser end of a pencil till she gets it down to the penny.

She is a housewife.

The next morning, my father takes me into his office. It's a beautiful room—red walls, cedar ceiling, deep leather Eames chairs where the shrink and patient sit.

"Take it easy with Erica," my father says gently. "She's having a rough time."

Later that day, when they are out, I search my mother's dresser. I don't know what I'm looking for because I don't know what the question is, but I do find the answer: a small cardboard box with a gold lid. It's hidden under a scarf and filled with Seconal— maybe twenty red capsules, bright as blood.

So I am not the only one filching downers from my father.

Hours after I bring him her suicide stash, she takes one careful step into my room. "I am really sorry," she says somberly, "you had to find that." She says, "I don't know why I felt compelled to stockpile those pills. But I want you to know I never planned to take them."

It's a speech, and she has come to the end of it.

She has one hand on the doorknob, and I don't know how to swim to her or if I even want to.

"It's okay," I say.

It is 1947 and my mother is twenty. She has quit the University of Miami and moved to New York, and for an easy few months she lives rent-free on West 114th Street, in a building owned by her father, Ulrich. Once he managed Miami hotels and Borscht Circuit resorts; now he is in a wheelchair. He depends on his second wife, who dislikes my mother, to feed him, bathe him, help him to the john. And Ulrich is weak in other ways. He has never stood up for his baby girl. When Erica was little, and asthmatic, her mother would charge to her bed at night with a hairbrush in her raised hand and hiss, "Stop. That. Coughing," until her daughter learned to choke it back.

Esther's violence was a force as unstoppable for him as his own stroke. But he's told Erica, I've made it up to you, sweetheart. When I'm gone, you'll be set.

And so my mother is shocked to find herself homeless, cut off, on his death a few months later. "Because my daughter, Erica Ellner, has displeased me in ways she will recall and understand," the lawyer says, eyeing her over his glasses, "I leave her the sum of four thousand dollars." The rest of the estate—and there is a lot of it, including the building where she lives—goes to her stepmother.

It's a new will.

"She forced him to sign that," my mother says through her fingers. "Can I sue?"

"Not if you're already in his will," the lawyer says. "That's the purpose of the four thousand dollars. You understand? Now you can't say he disinherited you."

Thanksgiving 1976. Erica is in her study, sorting through papers, which somehow creates a mess she cannot corral, which utterly confounds her. Then her daughter asks if she can take the oil portrait for her dorm room.

"Please do," says Erica. "I'm so tired of looking at it." It's that tinge of regret in the painting that gets her. She's moved on, but the woman in the picture has not.

She adds, "When I was a young woman, I modeled for the Art Students League."

"*Really*," her daughter says. She has an encouraging way of hanging on Erica's stories without prying. "Did you save any of the work?"

"No. But I did walk by once and see my portrait in the window."

As she talks, she moves a sheaf of brown envelopes from a

manila folder into a liquor carton and tucks them into place. She does this as if this were meaningless household work and not the concealment of a dozen unopened—never mind uncashed—Medicare reimbursement checks for her husband's psychotherapy work.

The idea is that she deposits each check in the bank, enters the amount into a business spreadsheet, and squares everything up. Debits, credits, categories. But she cannot square things up. So she buries the checks, like a squirrel.

Her daughter gets excited. Well, of course, they both know the building. It's beautiful, French Renaissance style, with tall and prominent display windows.

"Did you go in and try to buy it?"

"No," says Erica. "I could use some help in the kitchen."

"You didn't track down the artist?"

"Not that interested, I suppose."

"In your *own portrait?*"

Erica tucks in the flaps of the carton. It bears typed labels that say CLOTHES FOR DONATION. "Come help me cut green beans," she says.

The carton must have a thousand, two thousand dollars of checks in it by now. Soon she will start a new one. How does one get rid of such things?

The Bill Rivers story is a parasitical worm that swims beneath her skin.

• • •

In 1946, Bill Rivers comes to New York and studies at the Art Students League for three years.

In 1947, my mother begins to model there.

She is twenty-one, fatherless, and evicted. She moves as far from West 114th Street as she can get, to a town house smack where Minetta Street runs into Minetta Lane.

The apartment is small and dark, but the building is a frosted cake. She gets a job selling ads for the Yellow Pages over the phone, and sells more ads than anyone in her office, using her bright-but-serious voice.

For pin money, she models at the Art Students League.

The studio smells deliciously of turpentine, though when she sees that most of the students are men, she stands quite still holding her pocketbook. Then the instructor sees her and says, "Thank you for coming to our workshop," as if she were a visiting artist.

He hands her a folded white sheet and directs her to a standing screen.

My mother takes off her clothes quietly. Nude modeling for the purposes of art is not erotic. She knows this. It's a job. She *knows* this. She looks down at her body, which is sexy and curvy when she's dressed but maybe not so lovely when she's naked. Her breasts are perky, but the nipples are inverted—slightly pursed at the tips. Her doctor says she will have to bottle-feed when the time comes.

My mother wraps herself in the sheet and walks out with her shoulders erect.

She is good at holding a pose. She is good at finding the pose again after a break. She is good at noticing, from the corner of her eye, how the young men might as well be medical students the way they study her body, probing with their gazes for line, light, shadow.

And maybe she thinks that one of them notices through his eyelashes when she robes herself; and because she thinks he is exceptionally handsome, she takes her time arranging the sheet, and stops to look at how he's portraying her.

Not till it's finished, he says, and blocks her view. *Haywood Rivers. Call me Bill*. He holds out his hand. *A pleasure painting you, Erica*.

My mother closes her eyes. *Let me guess*, she says. She watches films like a critic and has an uncanny ear for accents. Just by listening at the movies, she's erased her own New York twang. *One of the Carolinas*, she says, and that is just the first time she cracks him up.

It's April 1992, and the magnolia in my parents' side yard is showing off blossoms big as salad plates. My little boy is in the living room playing with trains, ignoring the narrative my father is trying to concoct.

Upstairs, my mother tells me and my husband what sounds like the end of the Bill Rivers story. We're in her cluttered study. It's cozy, my mother's version of gathering around a hearth.

She tells us he gave her a painting.

"You had a Bill Rivers painting?" My husband looks almost

covetous. He is interested in African American art—very interested; we have begun, at a low level, to collect it. He knows exactly who Haywood Bill Rivers is. "Where is it?"

"After we lost touch," my mother says, "I tried to sell it."

We are amazed, my husband because he can't believe my family would let go of such a thing, me because when you and your friend are so close you have pet names for each other, why would you turn around and sell the painting he gave you?

My mother goes on: "I read that Harry Abrams had a big collection of work by black artists. So I called him. I told him what I had, and he said, Bring it in."

She recognizes many of the artists whose paintings hang in Harry Abrams's office. She works now at the Metropolitan Museum, in Permissions, and spends her lunch hour strolling through the galleries.

He looks at the painting, at her, at the painting, and, she says, lowballs her.

"Thank you for your time," my mother says, and takes her painting home.

My husband and I eye each other. She knew the work had value.

"So where is it?" I say.

"It got damaged in a move," my mother says vaguely, as if a move had inflicted itself upon the painting without her knowledge.

"Damaged how?" I ask.

"I don't remember." Her hand waggles through the air, indicating that the episode has dissipated like so much smoke.

"How damaged?" my husband asks.

My mother shrugs. "Probably badly."

My husband and I exchange looks again. "Paintings can be restored," I say, and leave the rest hanging—you hung out with artists, you worked in a museum, you knew that. "So what happened to it?"

My mother's hand floats out again. So much smoke. "I threw it away."

The Bill Rivers story is a parasitical worm that swims beneath my skin.

He's been thinking about Paris almost since that sheet fell from her like a chrysalis. Half the painters he respects are in Paris or going there. Beauford Delaney. Ed Clark. Lois Mailou Jones, who has some balls for a woman, going alone.

Often they go to Stanley's. Erica fits right in. She's a finely tuned listener, and when she has something to add, her intelligence glitters. There is talk of a new gallery being formed in Paris by some of the black expat artists, and he wants to paint modern paintings now, and be a part of it.

He brings Erica's painting to Minetta Lane. *Do you like it?* he says, and he genuinely wants to know.

He watches her carefully study the intricate pattern but also the chunks of light, the blocks of color. This is the end of his figurative period, the churches, the aunts. The portraits from his classes. He's aware of that.

I love this, she says at last. *And it means so much to me to have it.*

And then, or sometime after, one of two things happens.

Either he asks her—and she blows it.

Or else he never asks her at all.

In May 1983 I phone home with my news.

My fiancé and I hold the phone together, in the bright doorway of our balcony. We live in the French Quarter of New Orleans, and we're both reporters for the *Times-Picayune*—he's investigative, I'm medical.

He is black. I am white.

He feels strongly that I should wait and do this in person. I don't understand his reservations. I am twenty-seven years old. I love my parents. I can't wait.

I am ignorant.

My father answers and I tell him and he says, "This is the best news you could give me, honey. If I had to handpick my son-in-law, I would pick him." Then I hear him bellow up the stairs for my mother.

To my amazement, when I tell her, she lets a long silence unspool till I am unsettled. This is a woman who fed me books by Alice Walker, Richard Wright, Toni Morrison—who brought me to the Broadway opening of *for colored girls who have considered suicide / when the rainbow is enuf.* Maybe that does not mean what I thought it meant.

Finally she says, "What about the children?"

I am twenty-seven. I am ignorant.

"What about them?" I say, angry and cavalier. "We aren't going to beat them."

In 1949, Bill Rivers goes to Paris, where he meets an American woman with a glinting mind and an incandescent smile. Her name is Betty Jo Robirds. She has a master's in English and a Fulbright, which has brought her to the Sorbonne. She is white.

Imagine that he takes Betty Jo to Les Deux Magots, where the expat writers and painters and musicians, black and white, drink excellent, cheap French wine. She fits right in, laughing along with everyone else, and when she talks she's funny and smart.

It is like being with Erica at Stanley's, but better because it's Paris, and he feels his artistic life opening here like a rare night-blooming flower.

One of the expat painters says, *Any word from Erica?* and he puts his arm around Betty Jo, who doesn't waste time worrying about what's not in front of her.

We've lost touch, he says.

When he asks her to marry him, Betty Jo doesn't ask, *What about the children?* But because France has laws against interracial marriage, they take a boat to England in 1951 and marry there.

They have a son first, then a daughter. *A perfect doll of a brown baby*, reports *Jet* magazine. Is she still managing to take classes at the Sorbonne? Bill works with paint so thick now, in ambers, blues, and muted greens, that some of his canvases can't even be rolled up and shipped back home.

When Betty Jo looks back later on the Paris years before their divorce, one obituary will say, she recalls "poverty, beauty, and happiness."

Or else he never asks my mother at all.

My mother has one more chapter to share. She reveals it to me when our son is ten, and I am alone with her again in that cozy, messy room.

She is walking in New York one day, many years after those days in the Village, when she hears her name called. Bill Rivers is walking toward her, his face lit with recognition.

"Our eyes met," my mother says. "He saw instantly that I knew him. But I snubbed him, Dylan. I looked away as if he were a stranger, and I walked right past him."

My heart aches as if the person she had snubbed were me, or herself.

For the next twenty years and probably for the rest of my life, I will replay that moment, revising it, trying to get my mother's face to light up too. In this movie, I steer her into the embrace, into ardent conversation on the sidewalk as people flow around them, then the inevitable drink at—where are they? Fifty-Sixth

Street?—the Oak Room, and the beginning of a slow reversal in her life, aching and grieving, as radical and cataclysmic as when the Chicago River began its arduous turnaround and flowed the other way.

In this movie, Bill Rivers is a free man. My mother is not a free woman. But I'm not considering my father, who would be crushed, and lost. And I don't care about the younger me. All I want is for Yum to dance again.

"Why did you walk away?" I ask her in the study that day. I'm almost imploring her.

"I don't know why," she says. "I'm so ashamed of my behavior that day."

You do know why, I think. Of course you know.

"We could try to find him," I say. "We could look him up."

She brings her hand to her mouth.

"It would be too painful," she says. "Please don't."

I give her my word. I leave it alone.

I always leave it alone.

Bill Rivers dies in 2002. I won't find this out for years.

A year before Erica's death, when she is eighty-four and I am fifty-seven, I ask her a personal question, and it's the wrong one.

"You've spoken so often of Bill Rivers," I say. My mother looks at me brightly from her wheelchair. "He gave you a painting. You had this amazing . . . friendship. And I've always wondered."

My mother waits. She is still beautiful, though her hair has grayed rather than silvered, and her body slightly thickened. Her sweater hides a feeding tube, and her scarf a tracheostomy tube.

Deep breath. "Mom, were you and Bill Rivers intimate?"

I have asked her nurse to give us privacy. My mother can no longer live without a nurse. In the bedroom, my father slumbers, his own wheelchair nearby.

My mother straightens and shoots blue light at me.

"I am offended," she says, "that you would ask me this."

My father dies in May 2014 and my mother dies seven weeks later, just after a state of rapture in which she declares the following while I take frantic notes:

"Give your friends a message for me. I accept the miracle that is upon me. I accept the miracle that is upon me. I accept the pain with appreciation. I am the luckiest woman in the world." And, after a pause, "I think one of the worst things in the world is to be cynical."

My mother's Bill Rivers story is over.

But my Bill Rivers movie keeps playing in my head. It has two endings.

Imagine this.

The year is 1949. Peddlers sell fish and fresh corn on the street, and you can buy a suit with two pairs of pants.

Bill Rivers tells my mother he is going to Paris.

She's been waiting for this. She says nothing.

He says, *Come with me, Erica. It's Paris. It's magical. I can paint and you can study at the Sorbonne—anything you want.*

She says nothing. Her blue eyes are ocean now, not sky.

Come to Paris, he says. *Marry me.*

My mother says slowly: *Is it even legal there?*

He cocks his head and watches her carefully. *It's legal in England*, he says. *There's a boat.*

After a long, thin silence in which she murders every bodily urge to embrace him, she says, *What about the children?*

When he walks away, she feels she is standing on the edge of a grave.

Or else he doesn't ask her at all.

He tells my mother he is going to Paris.

She's been expecting this. She says nothing.

I'll miss you like crazy, Erica, he says. *Promise me you'll write.*

My mother nods. *Like crazy* does not express what she has come to feel over these past couple of years. She doesn't speak.

He says, *Come see me off next Saturday at the docks.*

My mother says slowly, *I'm afraid that won't be possible.*

He looks at her, puzzled. Then he understands. He nods and kisses her on the forehead.

When he walks away, she feels she is standing on the edge of a grave.

• • •

When my Bill Rivers movie plays, there is only ever one painting.

My mother, twenty-one or twenty-two, is the model, the muse. The portrait is a seated nude.

Haywood Bill Rivers is the artist. Because the painting is striking—its patterns are drawn from quilts made by the women of his family—it is displayed in a window of the Art Students League, where pedestrians on West Fifty-Seventh Street can see it. Of course my mother isn't curious who painted it. She knows.

They go to bars and to parties where artists and intellectuals meet. They become close enough for pet names, and Bill Rivers makes a gift of the portrait to her.

Perhaps two, three years after his ship sails, a mutual friend tells her that Bill Rivers is married in Paris, and not just married but to a white woman, a woman who's got what my mother would admiringly call spunk. This woman has studied at the Sorbonne, she's had a baby, maybe two, and she's friends with the very same expat artists my mother teased with that rapier wit of hers in New York—

My mother goes home to Minetta Lane and stands before the woman in the portrait. She tells her, *Betty Jo Rivers is living your life.*

Erica!

The voice of Bill Rivers that day on the street goes through my mother's heart like a stake.

Erica, he says. (She thinks he says.) Tell me, what did you do with your glittering mind?

Did you make the right choice? Marry the right man?

Would you have studied at the Sorbonne, Erica? Laughed with writers at Les Deux Magots?

Did you lock up that dazzling wit of yours, or did you write a book?

Did you get to stroll in Paris? Would you care if your daughter were a perfect doll of a brown baby?

Who would you love, Erica?

Who would you be?

In 2001, at my mother's request, I hide three mislabeled cartons of uncashed Medicare checks in our Santa Monica garage. She guesses there is $10,000 in those boxes. When we move out in 2007, they are gone. My parents live in Brentwood now, close by, so I ask my mother if she took them.

Her hand gesture is so much smoke in the air.

My husband discovers that a Haywood Bill Rivers painting, an early figurative work of a country church with a detailed choir in the loft, was auctioned as part of Mrs. Harry N. Abrams's estate on April 7, 2010. It brought $5,625.

I coax the doorman of my childhood building to let me explore the basement. Unbelievably, in 2012, people live in the once-padlocked storage rooms—I hear televisions through cracked-open doors and see shoes neatly outside.

In the laundry room, the screeching drying racks have vanished behind Sheetrock as if I had dreamed them, as if the orange-blue flames never burned.

After my mother dies in 2014, I make a pilgrimage to 16 Minetta Lane. I still desperately want to live there, because even though I am now fifty-eight, without a mother I am forever eight.

The house on Minetta Lane is no longer pink. Someone has taken the lantern down and painted the building white.

Fifteen

By Bernice L. McFadden

The first time I ran away from home was because your husband, my father, slapped me. He was drunk and I was fifteen years old. The blow was so hard; it sent me reeling into the closet. I remember cradling my stinging cheek with one hand, and using the other to shelter myself from the rain of clothing and metal hangers.

After I recovered from the shock, I crawled out of the closet, packed my suitcase, and left.

Outside, you rounded the corner, just home from a long day of work, and were stunned to see me lugging my suitcase toward a waiting taxi. You asked what was wrong, even though it was evident from the tears in my eyes and the angry red blotch on my cheek.

"I hate him," I screamed as the driver set my suitcase in the trunk of the car.

I climbed into the back seat and slammed the door, leaving you standing on the sidewalk wringing your hands.

I don't know what happened in the apartment that evening. I'm sure the two of you argued. I'm sure he called me disrespectful, accused me of talking back, of behaving as if I were better than him because I attended private school and my classmates were privileged white girls who spoke to their parents any old kind of way, and he wasn't going to tolerate that type of insolence from his black daughter.

I stayed with my best friend for three days and three nights. I did not call to let you know where I was or that I was safe.

My plan was to spend the next few weeks there and then head back to boarding school at the end of the summer. How exactly I was going to do that—sans money—I did not know.

On the morning of the fourth day, just as the night sky flaked away, the apartment bell buzzed. And then buzzed again—long and hard and angry.

I knew before my friend's mother peered through the peephole that he was on the other side of that door.

In the back seat of his car I bawled the entire ride home.

Over the years, I ran away again. He was still a drunk, and you still left and went back, left and went back. Whenever I asked why we didn't just stay gone, why we didn't just move in permanently with Grandma and Granddaddy; you would always seem wounded by my question. You'd just adjust your eyeglasses, shift your sad eyes from my probing ones, and mumble:

You don't know what your grandmother did. . . . One day. One day I'll tell you.

By the time I gave up waiting for you to leave him and waiting for you to tell me what I didn't know about my grandmother, I was nineteen years old, with a full-time job, a steady boyfriend, and my very own telephone line, which I paid for. Yes, I still lived under his roof, but I was no longer a child, muted by my age and dependency. I saw myself as a grown-ass woman. Now, when he barked, I barked back.

I was twenty-two years old when he was fired from the job he'd secured the year I was born. Three months later, I gave birth to a daughter of my very own. I had brought her into this world, but we would raise her together—she belonged to both of us— me and you, Mommy—she was my daughter, but she was our girl.

In 2001, our girl and I moved into my very own home. I felt safe leaving you there with him because the power structure had changed. You were now the head of the house, the breadwinner. All decisions began and ended with you. He had been reduced to a guest with squatter's rights.

I had been an obedient, respectful child and an obedient and respectful teenager. Our girl was different; she was outspoken and brazen in a way I never dared to be. She was more like you than me.

When she declared interest in a young man at her high school, I told her what you had told me at fifteen: *You can date at sixteen and not before.*

Had I not been sequestered away at an all-female boarding school, I might have defied that order, but she wasn't away; she was attending school right there in Brooklyn and took to lying about her whereabouts and cutting classes in order to spend time with the boy.

When I discovered this, I was angry, of course. I asked her if she was having sex and she vehemently denied it and then continued to defy me.

I threatened expulsion from my house. On the phone, I loudly berated her to friends and family, hoping to shame her into submission.

Look at the life she has; look at the home I've made for her.

I've taken her around the world and this is how she repays me? Selfish, what a selfish child she is. If I had what she has when I was growing up, I never would have given my parents a lick of trouble. In fact, I didn't have it and I still followed my parents' rules.

That boy don't care about her. She thinks she's in love. Sex ain't love; it just feels like love.

What an ungrateful child.

That only made things worse.

At my wits' end, I did something I vowed to never do. I read her journal, and in those pages, I discovered (as I had suspected) that she was having sex. I also learned that her teenage disdain for me had escalated to hatred.

When she came home from school, I confronted her, waving the journal in her face. I remember how the pages flapped, loud and ominous like the wings of so many blackbirds. When her normally stoic and unbothered facade crumbled into tears, I felt vindicated.

We went to our separate bedrooms and remained there, smoldering. When I woke the next morning, she was gone.

She'd left a letter, accusing me of intrusion and lacking of love and devotion.

I called her father and calmly told him that our daughter had run away. His response was a very weary sigh.

I knew the boy's first and last name and had his telephone number. The website ReversePhoneLookup.com gave me his address.

I called to tell you what was happening. And you were as upset about our girl running away as I remember you being whenever my father hit you.

While you traveled to my house by taxi, her father, a veteran NYC police officer, was banging on the door of the rooming house in which the boy lived.

Later, when my daughter was a woman and could speak freely about that time, she said that she and the boy were petrified, frightened mute by her raging father pounding the door so hard they thought it would collapse in on itself.

You arrived, followed by my sister and sister-in-law. We all gathered in the living room to worry over yet another splinter in an already fractured family.

The ordeal went on for hours. After her father left, the boy spirited our girl from one safe house to the next until finally some weary mother convinced her to go home and work things out with me.

Through much of the chaos, you had been particularly quiet and then when word came that she was on the way home, you turned to me and I saw that the expression on your face had changed from worry to alarm.

Promise me you won't send her to jail. Promise me.

What? I bleated. What are you saying? Why would I put her in jail?

You don't know what your grandmother did. . . . One day. One day I'll tell you.

That day had finally arrived.

I knew that you were born in 1943, just a few months before your mother turned sixteen. Not too long after you were born, she left for Chicago, escaping the racism and poverty of the South. But also to get away from the men in that house who believed they had as much right to the females who lived there as they did to the land they farmed.

When your mother was twenty-five and you were nine, she finally sent for you, because you were a big girl, already growing breasts.

You got to know her then, and from the beginning, you saw that she was a pathological liar and a thief.

The stealing and the lying started when she was a child. Her sister had stories about Thelma, about her light-fingered ways that followed her from childhood into adulthood. She'd stolen cherished photographs from family members and jewelry from her employers.

When I was in middle school, she supervised a team of custodians in a building that housed the corporate offices of a major financial institution. She gave me a ring that I wear to this day. A ring that she swiped from a safe left open in the office of an investment banker.

You told me about the time she discovered you were seeing an older boy. He'd given you two cashmere sweaters, which you'd hid in the bottom of your trunk. You came home from school and there she was, standing at the stove wearing those sweaters— both of them. You were shocked but didn't say a word and neither did she. She placed the food on the plates and brought it to the table. Over dinner you spoke about everything but those sweaters. Afterward, you washed the dishes, went into the bedroom, and cried. You never saw those sweaters again.

When you and my father were planning your wedding, he telephoned you demanding why you'd lied about being in love with him, why you'd told him that the baby you were carrying belonged to him when it was seeded by another man, and why hadn't you been woman enough to tell the truth to his face instead of sending it in a letter like a coward.

You had received a letter too.

A letter from him declaring his love for another woman, a woman who was pregnant with his child, a woman he intended to marry instead of you.

Neither of you had sent the other a letter. When you compared the handwriting, they matched. The postmark was stamped on the same day in the same zip code, 11420. The zip code in which you and my grandmother lived. She had sent those letters and denies it to this day.

The first time you shared these stories with me, I was too young to understand. But as I grew older, I saw the truth.

In Chicago, my grandmother left you before dawn to travel to her job as a domestic in a home in an affluent suburb. You were expected to get yourself up, dressed, fed, and off to school. Back at home, you finished your homework and started dinner. You were nine years old.

Eventually, you and she moved to Detroit and, finally, Brooklyn.

By then, you were a teenager.

The two of you had your battles. Battles that mothers and daughters have. But your mother never knew when to let things go. You said she never hit you, but you wished she had—because you would have preferred a slap to the nagging. You said sometimes the nagging went on for days. She'd rail on and on about the tiniest infractions: the tub wasn't clean enough, the carpet hadn't been swept properly. It seemed to you she just enjoyed making you miserable.

It was that badgering that drove you to run away in the summer of 1958. You were fifteen years old.

You tell me that back then, people in your community rarely finished high school. College was a place white people went. It was cause for celebration if a child graduated from middle school. Your own mother only went up to the fourth grade.

That was your plan. You were going to drop out of high school, find a job, rent a room, and never have to deal with her niggling ever again. The day your life changed, you were in a bar with friends—back then, teenagers went to bars and were served if they looked eighteen. You were mature for your fifteen years. Two men dressed in suits approached you, showed you gold badges, identified themselves as NYC detectives, and asked your name. You gave it, and they told you that you were being arrested for larceny. They handcuffed you, read you your Miranda rights, and hauled you away in the back of an unmarked police car.

As the story spills from your mouth, your brown eyes turn black, and I know you are back in 1958, in the dark back seat of that police car, frightened and fifteen.

The mind is as wonderful as it is wicked; it can choose to save us from our memories or bludgeon us with them. You were shuddering.

Your mother stood up in court and accused you of stealing

money and jewelry from her. Your mother stood up in court and lied.

You were sentenced to a year in Westfield Farm, a women's detention facility in Bedford Hills, New York.

Your mother came to visit you every weekend. She came to visit you as if you were away at summer camp. The two of you never once talked about what she had done, or why she had done it. Till that day and since, you two have never discussed it. It was like the cashmere sweaters all over again.

You knew our family was swimming in secrets, terrible secrets, that were too painful and shameful to discuss, and so they didn't. They kept silent about the uncle who'd raped and impregnated at least two of his nieces, the brother who'd fondled his sister, and that aunt who tried and failed to drown her child in bathwater.

So, when Grandma went to visit you in prison, she brought you cigarettes, candy, sanitary napkins, and magazines but not an explanation, and you didn't ask for one, because you knew the rules.

In May 1959, Gay Talese, the veteran journalist, visited the prison and wrote an article for the *New York Times* about the Westfield prisoners' exercise routine.

Twenty-five barefoot girls in shorts sat Buddha-style on the floor, their fingers snapping slowly, their heads and torsos swaying to the jungle beat of an African drum.

Years later, I would wonder if you were one of those barefoot girls.

The performing prisoners spent almost an hour leaping through the air, crawling on the ground and swinging their hips to a number of tunes, including a Les Baxter version of "Ritual of the Savage."

At the end of your sentence, you returned home. Your mother had a new man in her life—a man who she would marry. You never went back to school. You met my father, became pregnant, and married him, and then I was born. You went on with your life with that secret lodged in your heart like an ice pick. And then our girl ran away, and the ice pick slipped out, and finally you told me that thing you had been holding for forty-five years.

Promise me you won't send her to jail. Promise me?

The last time I'd heard that pleading in your voice I was seventeen years old and my father had a gun to your head. Hearing it then nearly broke me. Thinking about it now breaks me. But you don't like tears, so I held them until our girl came back and you went home, and then I cried for all of us.

Nothing Left Unsaid

By Julianna Baggott

By the time I was ten, I was my mother's confessor. My older siblings were teenagers or already out in the world. I was the only one left, and she was bored and a little lonesome—or maybe, for the first time, she had the bandwidth to reflect on her own life and childhood. She would keep me home from school to do banking, play casino, and tell me the darkest stories you've ever heard.

I remember these conversations happening on our screened-in porch while playing cards. This makes no sense, of course. We lived in Delaware, and most of the school year, it would have been too cold. But it's always late spring in my recollection. I can see my mother in a housedress, her red hair puffed up around her face. She's snapping cards down on the plastic tablecloth. Our neurotic dalmatian, Dulcie, is forever dipping in and out of the doggy doors—plastic flaps that my father nailed into place.

My mother kept me home if it was a rainy day, worried about the bus on the highway, but also on sunny days because it was too pretty to be cooped up. She kept me home on her birthday, which, by her reasoning, was far more important to me, personally, than any president's birthday. Sometimes she had no reason at all. She gave me the impression that school was beneath me. "Give the other kids a chance to catch up," she'd tell me, conspiratorially, as if my genius were a secret.

This wasn't true and I knew it. I was an average student, poor at math, never the strongest reader. Because of the absences, I was often lost in history and science. However, I learned something that became very useful—how to fake it.

We took the card games seriously, but we chatted a lot too. My mother had already raised three kids, and so I was more of a compadre. I was used to being spoken to like an adult. I hated it when other grown-ups treated me like a child. I was pretty sure that the rest of the world underestimated children, but my mother's confessions were proof that I, at least, could handle much more.

And when I tell you that the stories were dark, I mean it. There was the story of an aunt who had a home abortion with knitting needles; the baby lived for three days. In another story, one of my grandmother's aunts hanged herself from a bedpost.

And there were the stories that hit closer to home—my mother's father was abusive to my grandmother. My mother told me that, when she was little, she assumed that varicose veins were bruises left by violent husbands.

I don't recall her being tense or tearful while telling me the stories. I don't recall any big outpouring or rush of words. She was reflective, thoughtful. Sometimes I had the impression that she was saying these things aloud for the first time, as if the memories were dawning on her, unfiltered.

There were good stories too. My mother's devotion to the piano, her love for the kind nuns who helped her family time and again, her love affair with my father.

This story stands out in my memory. Her father couldn't read or write. From a meager background, he quit school at a young age and started making money as a pool-hall hustler. But one evening, while he was watering the grass, he asked her to tell him something she'd learned.

"I quoted Shakespeare," my mother said, and she recited this line: "Night's candles are burnt out, and jocund day stands tip-toe on the misty mountaintops." She took a moment and then added, "My father thought it was beautiful." My mother could sense a depth within him, a longing. "I imagine all the things that he could have done if his life had allowed it," she said.

My mother's side of the family seemed to believe that stories could save us. They were cautionary tales, medical wisdom, and lessons in love and loss.

. . .

For a while in my twenties and early thirties, I'd started to doubt the stories I'd heard from my mother. They were too mythic. How does one hang oneself from a bedpost?

Another story was nearly biblical. Our ancestors in Angier, North Carolina, set off one night in a storm—a man, a woman, and a baby on horseback. The man and the woman were killed in the storm, but the baby was found, wrapped in a grapevine, alive!

I was a grown woman with children of my own by this point. I'd studied the Southern gothic in graduate school. I knew lore when I heard it.

One day, in my mother's kitchen, my father was doing some genealogy. He was fastidious in his work—only the facts. My mother found it boring, which seemed to me like an admission of guilt that she'd spiced her own family's stories.

So I called her on it, in particular, the hanging. "It doesn't make sense logically," I said. "And it's just too dramatic."

She refused to give in. We fought about it. Eventually, she seemed to give in a little. "Fine," she said. "You don't have to believe me."

I went home—living only a mile away at that point—feeling like I'd won.

That evening, my mother walked into my house holding a newspaper clipping that had been saved in the family Bible. Written in the deep Southern gothic tradition that I knew so well, it included the aunt's blind, invalid mother who, in the next room, could do nothing to help and had to listen to her daughter choke to death. "What do you think of the story now? Do you still think I made it up?"

I conceded.

When the baby found in the grapevine was also corroborated, years later, in a small self-published history of the area of Angier, I gave up. By this point, I was a novelist. And it had dawned on me, of course, that hearing these stories may have, in part, made me a writer or, at the very least, honed my aesthetic. It's no surprise that I'm drawn to magical realists and fabulists, that I love a touch of absurdism. On the one hand, I'm not sure it was perfect mothering to tell me these stories at such a young age, but it might have been the exact kind of mothering that a budding novelist could mull and eventually spin something from. By the time I was in my early thirties, having published my first two novels, I decided it was time to write part of my family's history.

Another true story: My grandmother had been raised in a house of prostitution in Raleigh, North Carolina, during the Great Depression. Her mother was the madam of the house. This had been kept from my mother throughout her childhood; my mother was the only one who didn't know. In fact, it was my father who told her when, still newlyweds, he heard about it in those slow, drawling conversations that only the men of the family had out on the porch. It shocked my mother, but it also made complete sense, as is so often the case with long-held secrets.

To be clear, I too have come to believe that telling family

stories—letting them air out—is the healthiest way to live. My father came from a tight-lipped family. His father died when he was five years old—an Army jeep accident—and he didn't know until decades later, when he was in his forties, that his mother had left his father about a year and a half earlier. She had scribbled a note in their Brooklyn apartment and hauled her three children back to West Virginia, alone.

This seemed deeply unhealthy to me, and when I married a WASP, tight lips running throughout *his* family tree, I evangelized the importance of not having any secrets, telling it all. His own childhood was fractured by divorce, and so he was down for trying a different approach.

At this point, my grandmother was in her eighties and not in perfect health. I knew that, in order to get firsthand accounts of her childhood, I needed to write the story right away, even though I didn't feel quite ready enough.

With a mini tape recorder, I sat down with my grandmother in her pink condo, with her poodle in her lap, and started interviewing her. She had a wonderful childhood, she told me. She loved her mother and father. She had fond memories of the women in the house. The men would give her nickels to go to the movies. But when her mother went off with a man, she and one of her brothers were sent to the orphanage for brief stints. And by fifteen, it was clear she could no longer live in a house of prostitution; it was too dangerous. So she married her brother's best friend, my grandfather. When he beat her up the first time, she got on a bus and went home. The part of the story I couldn't bear—and still can't—is that her mother sent her back to him.

I learned quickly that my grandmother was fine with doing the interviews, but I wasn't. I found it difficult. I would get emotional and have to go to her pink bathroom, splash water on my face, and collect myself.

Eventually, I taught her to use the tape recorder and talk into it, deep into the night, the hours when she was often wide awake. This way, I could listen to the tapes and stop them when I couldn't go on any longer.

And now there were things that my grandmother told me not to tell my mother, not many, but they were notable. And so I became a vault between them.

While my grandmother's health was failing, there was a moment when she said to my mother, "There's something I haven't told you." It was clear that it was something important, something that she needed to tell my mother before she died. By this point, there was little left unsaid. The stories my mother had told me had been passed down to her—and there were too many to keep track of. My research had unearthed a lot of what had been quietly buried. Others in the family of storytellers had lived long lives and confessed more as they aged.

My mother says that she drew in a breath and thought, *Oh my. Here we go.* She explains her apprehension this way: "My mother had told me so much. She was so honest. I was sure she hadn't held back. I couldn't imagine what she'd spared me, and I was afraid of what she would say."

In that brief moment, my grandmother looked at her daughter and read her expression, a mix of fear and maybe weariness. After that one moment of surprise, she said, "Well, maybe there are some things you don't need to know."

My mother was relieved. She was thankful, in fact, that she and her mother were so close that there was that quick moment of unspoken communication.

My mother returns to this moment from time to time. Did she deny her mother something? Did she ask her mother for a final kindness and was that the true gift—not telling?

"I admit that sometimes I wonder what it could have been, but I don't regret it," my mother says. My mother was an only child. My grandmother had her when she was just seventeen. They were mother and daughter, but they also grew up together. They loved each other as deeply as two people can.

I think about my father's mother—the one who left that note for her husband and took her children back home to the mountains. Their father died. Why tell them that the marriage was over? Why tell them that he blew his paychecks on drinking and left them with little to scrape by? He was also wonderful in his way. Why not let them have the few memories that would stick—his perfectly timed pratfalls, his dancing, his easy smile? Why muddy any of that? There's beauty and strength in letting them have their father—exactly as they wanted and needed him to be.

Like my ancestors, I believe that stories can save us. Our stories are our greatest currency. What one person is willing to share with another is a test of intimacy, a gift that's given. Some people might see my mother's confessions as a burden she lifted off of her own shoulders to put onto mine. I don't. I see them as moments of shared humanity. She was lifting the veil of politeness, of the quotidian, and she was real and vulnerable in those moments. She was honest about who she was and those who came before us. No matter how dark the stories were, they were hopeful. The storyteller is a survivor, after all. *I lived to tell the tale* is not an idle saying. My mother was giving voice to the past, to those who couldn't tell their own stories. Storytelling is a fight against forgetting, against loss and even mortality. Every time a story is told about someone who's dead, it's a resurrection. Every time a story is told about the past, we're doubly alive.

Look, as a kid, I knew that what I was experiencing, day in and day out, wasn't the whole truth. All kids sense this. I was being protected from something. My mother let me glimpse behind that insulation. It was a comfort to have someone acknowledge that the rosy childhood that our culture clings to isn't real. She showed me that life is complex and rich—dark, yes, but also stunningly beautiful.

My mother is still telling me stories, new ones that surprise me. These days, there are more about her long marriage to my father. They're love stories, a little racy sometimes. My parents are in their early eighties, both still healthy. Now, looking back on my childhood, I'm thankful for all of the stories she's told me, not only as a writer but also for the closeness that's come from telling me her stories.

And, I admit, that I tell my older children some of the family stories as well. My oldest daughter, Phoebe Scott, is now twenty-three and a sculptor who does life-size sculptures of women's bodies, in particular the bodies of elderly women who wear their stories in their bones and on their skin. The family stories seem to fuel her work in ways that are similar and very different from my own.

Still, there's something that worries me. If my grandmother had held on to something until her deathbed, my mother might have this power, too.

Every once in a while, it hits me—what if she hasn't told me everything? What if the worst is still out there? What if there is one more thing?

If that moment comes and she whispers that she has to tell me something before she dies, I won't say no. I won't have the willpower. I'll have to know.

I'll lean down—even though perhaps I shouldn't—and I'll say, "What is it? Tell me."

The Same Story About My Mom

By Lynn Steger Strong

There is a story of my mother that I trot around as an antidote to other stories that I tell about my mother. I have, over the years, used it both to show how she is good as well as how I think that she is bad. I trade in stories maybe, but I think most of us do this. We pick the stories; we curate them; we pass them on to prove things either about us or about the people who they hold inside.

This story about my mother involves a weekend that she came up to move me out of my freshmen college dorm room. I was eighteen, a Depressed Person, and spent most of the time that she was there asleep in my bed or in a chair at the library. For that whole time my mother cleaned my dorm room, did my laundry, sweat then showered then took me out to dinner. I was a Messy

Depressed Person and there had been, for months, a stench so strong emanating from the room that people smelled it in the hallways, asked about it, knew to avoid me mostly, looked at me and maybe talked about me, the few times a day when I left my room to use the bathroom or to shower.

My roommate had long ago moved out, exhausted by me surely, but also, she had been caught selling weed out of our room. Solitude had made the room even worse; there were piles of laundry, mostly sugar-crusted sweatpants and sweaty running clothes, cans of Betty Crocker icing, which was most of what I ate then, wrappers from the other junk foods that I binged on, wrappers from the burritos one of my friends used to bring me, in the weeks when I refused to leave the dorm.

My parents are relatively well-off, and I have told this story sometimes to show the ways in which my mother is much more than her fancy house and car and all the diamonds in her ears and on her wrists and fingers. I've told it to show she came from nothing; she loves me; she works hard. I've told it to show all the ways in which I was a useless, spoiled child of privilege. How I sat there. How she did load after load of laundry, making friends with the sophomore boys I'd mostly been afraid to speak to, when one of the coin machines broke and they gave her quarters, when she got them candy from the vending machine as thanks. Once, the next fall, she would carry a chair I'd liked and she had bought at Urban Outfitters on the subway all the way back to my dorm.

I have told it to show how hard it must have been to be my mom.

For years, I told this as a story of her strength. After I had kids, I twisted it. It twisted, as perhaps all of me twisted when I had kids. I was angry at my mother for a good portion of those first years that I myself was a mother.

She didn't talk to me, I told someone, holding one of my babies, nursing, which she didn't do when she had children, telling that same story of my freshman dorm room. *She didn't crawl up onto my dorm bed and talk to me*, I said. *She didn't ask me what was wrong.*

She knew what was wrong because I had sporadically been in therapy for years by then, because of all the shit I'd gotten up to in high school: alcohol poisoning and car accidents, skipping so much school that I had to be withdrawn. I had been prescribed all sorts of medication. I had refused to take them. She had yelled at me, cried at me, raged at me—I was useless, worthless, a piece of shit, what the fuck was wrong with me—sat in my room trying to hold me though I was bigger than her—please, please, please, please, please over and over—begging me to stop.

For a while when I had a toddler and I was pregnant, my mother and I stopped talking. We'd been fighting. She'd been yelling at me on the phone one day about my abominable life choices—the state and location of our Brooklyn apartment, a home in Florida that we were thinking of buying that was in immeasurable disrepair— as I stood, pregnant for the second time, outside a graduate class. Something shifted then in our fighting.

Now she was disparaging not only me but choices my husband and I were making for our children, not only my life but the life we were trying to create for them. We yelled at one another. There was no right or wrong or in between. At stake for both of us was whether or not we had been, or were now, loving our kids. Loving them the right way. After months of this fighting back and forth, I need a break, I told her. I wanted not to fight awhile and that had become all we ever did.

At that point my story changed again. I chose then to say that if I were my mother up in Boston that time she came to get me when I was still an adolescent, hardly functional Depressed Person, I would have forced me to tell her what was wrong with me. I would have talked to her, I said. I would have mothered *better*, I thought then and said out loud to other people, as if better were so clean and clear as imagining what she must have felt like then.

I am very good at stories. Like my mother, who is a lawyer, a litigator. I am also, like my mother, good at indignation. I'm good at feeling fury toward a thing or person by which or whom I feel I have been wronged. There is a sort of thrill that comes from it just below the surface of my anger or my sadness. It feels athletic, engaging. I gesture broadly and stand up tall.

When I was sixteen, my car got towed and my mother drove me, yelling the whole time about how disgusting I was, how awful, what a worthless piece of shit, to the tow lot to retrieve my car.

She told me in this yelling—which she did then often, which I had come, over months, to refer to as my fuck-up speech—they would not waste their hard-earned money on sending me to college. (This was not true, even she knew; they would never allow themselves to have a child not in college. This was just a thing she said during this talk she gave.) She told me she felt helpless, tired, how could I, why did I. I'd gained weight, I'd stopped showing up to school or track practice. I was drinking all the time and getting caught.

She drove with her red car's top down as she yelled at me. When we got to the tow yard, there were piles of cars stacked in the lot. The man told my mom she owed him six hundred dollars. She looked at me. I was in cotton pajama pants and a sweatshirt. My eyes were swollen from crying just minutes before. My face was swollen from the weight I'd gained. None of my clothes fit and this was what I wore as often as I could. No matter it was hot out. No matter that my skin pricked all over with little sweat bubbles that then settled back into my pores and gave off a smell that often made me sick.

My mother lit into this man, who was, as far as I could tell, just an employee of this car lot. I will sue you, she said. She explained to him the injustice of this thing he'd done, towing my car, a sixteen-year-old, a child, she said, who couldn't, didn't need to know, what she had done. To exploit us, she said, of six hundred dollars. She gestured toward me; to exploit this child, she said. She hung on the last word for emphasis. I cowered, partially out of fear, but also because I knew this was my role. She threatened to call the papers. She would file a civil suit against the lot for all the cars that he had piled up outside. She cited statutes. It's robbery, holding people's possessions hostage for these sums, she said.

The man, who was large, half-asleep when we entered, with stubble and a flash of belly sticking out from the bottom of his shirt, let her talk, then said we could take the car and to please just go now. When she handed me the keys, I watched her face change shape as she remembered we were only on the same team for as long as it took to get what we wanted.

This is supposed to be an essay about what I can't tell my mother, what I haven't told her. When I was asked to do this, I had that initial thrill of showing all the ways she makes me mad. But that didn't feel new or right or like it held inside most of what I feel any longer when I think of her. I have told her most of what I think. I have hurt her. She has hurt me. None of this feels secret.

The other day, I was teaching a gender studies class—nine teenage girls all anxious to say the right thing, their desks in a circle—and my students and I were talking about mothers. We were talking about the impossible positions they are placed in, the ways in which they are our models; we were talking about what little space moms have to also need and also want. My students didn't notice but I started crying. I teared up, and when the class was over, I went into a bathroom stall and sat until I stopped. I hadn't spoken to my mother recently. We don't speak often. I couldn't locate the specific feeling I'd had the last time we talked. I thought for a few hours after I cried in the bathroom that I would call her and I would tell her I loved her. But I did not trust calling her. I was afraid that if I called her, she would talk and it would be too hard for me to love her after that.

What I cannot tell my mother is whatever I would have told her on that phone call, on all the phone calls in which I take out my phone and scroll to her name, stare at it, and then put the phone away. There is a gaping hole perhaps for all of us, where our mother does not match up with "mother" as we believe it's meant to mean and all it's meant to give us. What I cannot tell her is all that I would tell her if I could find a way to not still be sad and angry about that.

Our younger daughter nursed much longer than I expected, until she was nearly two. I loved the ease of it, giving to her. She'd cry, I'd offer her a boob. She'd settle in, and all was good again. When I stopped nursing, I was afraid all of a sudden. All at once, there was no clear, clean way to give to her, no certain way to ensure that she'd calm down. When she needed, wanted, suffered, I had only my best guess: words, hugs, begging, asking, holding. I only had the flawed and abstract way that humans love.

I once had a therapist tell me I was just born to the wrong family. The "just" is hers, not mine. *We have different values* is a thing I sometimes tell people when they ask about my parents, but that sounds already more subjective, more judgmental, than I mean. We are very different, very separate people, who have both accidentally and on purpose hurt and loved one another poorly and intensely my whole life. As I get older, as I mother longer, this feels both just as fresh and white-hot hard as it did when I was fourteen. It also feels like almost every other life.

The other day, I let my kids watch TV while I cleaned the bathroom. I hardly ever do this. My mother let me watch loads of TV when I was little. After she had spent a full week working, providing for us in ways I have so far failed to provide for my kids, she often spent the weekend cleaning for us in ways I often fail to make our home clean for our kids. Back then I resented a thousand things about this for a thousand reasons, not least of what it said about what I would have to do when I was grown up, not least because I thought there might be other ways to love and to be loved.

But I did this same thing a couple of weeks ago. I was tired. They need more often than they don't need. They're at the age when they can sit in front of the TV for hours. I cleaned the bathroom because I wasn't up for all the complicated ways I would have to love them and entertain them if we turned off the TV and spent the day together. I hardly ever clean the bathroom and it was gross. Getting the mold out of the grout, scrubbing the soap scum off the bottom of the tub, my hands covered in bleach, my knees sore; it felt like giving to them in a way that was both familiar and substantial; it felt like what they needed, how I wanted to be a mother; it also felt like my mom.

. . .

Like so many days before this, I almost called my mother this day. In the mirror, too-thin arms and lots of freckles on the shoulders, a broad nose, short hair, sweat across my brow, I looked so much like her; I felt so much like her and I wanted to tell her how. But I have made that phone call and it has failed me too many times. She has not wanted to unpack or parse through our sameness, if only because I always start with wanting to address the ways that we have grown apart. She does not much like to talk about her feelings. She gets anxious when I ask her to consider what there is and is not behind and between us; she almost always feels attacked.

What I cannot tell my mother is that she hurt me and I'm angry, but it doesn't matter as much any longer. We all hurt one another. She could not not have hurt me. She could not not have made me angry. What I wish that I could tell her is that I am, finally, okay with that.

While These Things /
Feel American to Me

By Kiese Laymon

I'm a nine-year-old day camper at one of Jackson State University's summer programs. Renata, one of your students, is a twenty-one-year-old camp counselor. She is the only person I know at the camp. The first day of camp, all the campers get physicals. Next to my weight on the form, the camp doctor writes in scattered cursive the word "obis." I ask some older twins if their physicals say "obis" too.

"That means obese, nigga," one of them says. "It means you way too fat for your age."

I look up "obese" when I get home. My babysitter comes over. When she leaves, I feel less obese.

The second day of camp, I tell the twin who said I was obese that I've seen Renata, the camp counselor everyone says is finer than Thelma Evans, naked. "You think she look good now?" I remember saying. "She look way better without no shirt on."

When one of the twins tells me that there's no way Renata would ever be naked around an "obese lil nigga" like me, I describe a birthmark in the middle of Renata's chest. The twins suck their teeth but eventually tell some older boys who tell some older boys who tell some older boys. Before the end of the week, a large portion of the camp is calling Renata a "skeezer" behind her back.

And to her face.

Renata and I do not talk at camp. She goes out of her way to avoid me. I go out of my way to be avoided. But two nights of that week, like two nights a week during the previous few months, Renata comes to our house. Renata is technically my babysitter. She adores you. When Renata comes over, we watch wrestling. We read books. We play Atari. We drink Tang. Renata does rough things to my body. Those rough things make me feel chosen, loved. Renata acts like these rough things make her feel like she feels chosen, loved too. One day, I will see and hear Renata doing rougher things with her real boyfriend. I will hear Renata tell him to stop. The things he does to her will not sound like they make Renata feel chosen or loved. I will not care about what he is doing to Renata. I will care that Renata does not want to choose me anymore.

Over thirty years later, 160 miles from where Renata and I met, I remember the taste, temperature, and texture of the Tang

I drank right before Renata put her right breast in my mouth the first time. I remember the pressure she used to close my nostrils. I remember what her left palm did to my penis. I remember the way I flexed and clenched my body tightly when she touched my skin, not because I was scared, but because I wanted Renata to think my fat black soft body was harder than it really was.

I don't think I spread that rumor because of anything Renata did to my body. I spread that rumor because she was an older black girl, and I knew that spreading rumors about black girls, no matter their ages, was how black boys, no matter our ages, told each other I love you.

Over thirty years later, on days when my body and mind are most raggedy, I want to congratulate myself for not being Kavanaugh, Trump, or Cosby. I want to source my harmful behavior and annihilated relationships solely to my childhood experiences of sexual violence, or solely to economic lack, or solely to the ways of white folk, or solely to getting beaten, or solely to Mississippi needing black children to be grateful for the ways we were terrorized. My experience in this nation, in my state, in my city, in all sorts of American rooms, is far too funky, too smudged, too reliant on—and influenced by—concentric circles of violence to say that I harmed anyone in this country simply because of a singular experience of harm. I also can't say anyone in this country harmed me because of a singular experience of childhood harm.

None of us living in this nation are that lucky.

I've been thinking a lot this year about the importance of the word "while" when thinking about cause and effect in America.

"While" is a word you use a lot. Black feminists and Black Political Scientists have been trying to teach us to embrace "while" for decades. While Renata was harming me in a way I could not harm her, I was harming her in a way she could not harm me. Meanwhile, sexual violence in our communities was happening while domestic violence was happening, while economic inequality was happening, while mass evictions and mass incarceration were happening, while states were failing and abusing teachers, while teachers were failing and abusing students, while abused students were abusing themselves and their younger siblings.

Last year, I finished a piece of art I started for you at twelve years old. I wanted to artfully explore the shape and consequences to our bodies of not reckoning with so many familial and national secrets. You agreed that I should call that piece of art *Heavy*.

After the ninth draft of *Heavy*, with some urging, I understood that it is beyond maniacal to harm someone who loved me privately, and then publicly atone for that harm I've done to that person in a publication for cheap male-feminist points and corporate money. While I have been harmed and abused as a kid, I have never had to experience watching someone publicly narratively confess to abusing me because they too were abused for money.

This might change tomorrow, but today the most important question in my world is: What do I really want to lie about? Am I willing to not simply answer that question, but reckon with the interpersonal and structural consequences of the question and our lies? Why do I really want to lie? Why did we lie to each other so much, for so long? And how will I react when called on those lies? I still desperately want to lie about the harm and abuse I've inflicted on people who loved me. I still desperately want to believe that I don't initiate romantic relationships because I've always been a decent guy, not because I've always been a fat black boy terrified of rejection, terrified of not being chosen. I still want to believe that breathtaking literary work necessitates American men sentimentally naming the hurt we've done, sourcing that hurt to one trauma, and getting congratulated, often by women, for "our honesty" at reckoning with that trauma while neglecting the suffering we cause. I still desperately want to believe that a haphazard collection or cataloguing of cherry-picked confessions is what makes art last. I know it doesn't.

But, I still want to lie.

I finished revising the memoir I started writing to you on my grandmama's porch at twelve years old, not because I wanted to chronicle the journey of becoming, but because I couldn't lie anymore about what I'd become. I'd become a cowardly, lonely, unhealthy, emotionally abusive, addicted, successful black writer. In writing the book, I discovered that I'd never been honest with anyone on earth. I discovered that while structural abuses dictate much of our lives, the folks I've been most harmful to in this country are people I thought I loved. I discovered that there are lovers in this country who honestly, rigorously, and generously love while being targeted, harmed, and manipulated by people, by institutions, by policy.

There are teachers who do all they can to understand the style and context of their students' lives while ethically educating them without harming them. There are members of boards of trustees and regents who risk their jobs by placing the health of vulnerable people ahead of an institution's bottom line. There are parents who make every decision in life with a concern about how it impacts not just their child, but all vulnerable children on earth while not having enough money to pay for health care, bus passes, and food for themselves.

But the truth is, in America, there are few of these folks.

Or maybe we choose to believe we are these kind of Americans far too often. I know I do. And if, as I believe, this choice is really the bedrock of American terror, then reckoning with this choice must be at the root of any semblance of liberation in this country. I know, after finishing this project, the problem in this country is not that we fail to "get along" with people, parties, and politics with which we disagree. The problem is that we are horrific at justly loving the people, places, and politics we purport to love. I wrote *Heavy* to you because I wanted us to get better at love.

After reading *Heavy*, you wrote back to me:

In my remembrance, I hear our laughter, our arguments, my incessant worry about your safety, your good grades through fifth grade; all your basketball games in rural outposts, your choices in girlfriends, the New Orleans and Memphis trips, the underdogs, and yes, the fear that I'd lose you too early, either because you would turn your back on me or be shot from the sky. I lived in fear, when, perhaps, I should have willed myself to live with more courage, less tough love, and more conviction. I took some of the wrong chances.

When Renata ran out of my house nearly naked with her boyfriend over thirty years ago, my heart broke. I felt like I'd lost the love of the second grown woman who chose me. I now know that I did not love Renata. I loved how Renata made me feel. I'm not sure I loved you. I know I loved how you sometimes made me feel. Even if Renata was choosing to harm me, at least she wanted to touch me. For reasons completely American, that rough touch felt like love to me because she could have been roughly touching any other black child in our neighborhood. For reasons completely American, I did not think about the abuse Renata was experiencing, not just from her boyfriend or her parents or her teachers, but from all boys in our world and me. Now that I have thought about all of it, and shared it with you, how will we allow all of it, all the whiles, any of the whiles, to make us better at loving us backward and forward? That is the only question that matters to me right now. Can you tell me what questions matter to you? Can we spend the rest of our lives talking about those questions? Can we please get better at loving each other in America?

Mother Tongue

By Carmen Maria Machado

A few months before my wife, Val, and I got married, we decided to see a nonreligious couples counselor for a set of sessions meant to prep us for a life together. We wanted to start things off right—look for what we were missing, gather tools to help us succeed. Our therapist—an astute, hysterically funny woman named Michelle—was, I thought, precisely what we needed. She was thoughtful and found a way to artfully cut through each of our defenses—Val's emotion, my retreat from it. (Recognizing what two oldest children needed from her, she gave us endless praise for our hard work, and a certificate when we ultimately graduated.) When we came to the discussion about children—there was an entire session dedicated to it, the premarital counseling version of Shark Week—I was surprised to find myself expressing ambivalence to parenthood.

Val and I had talked about children, of course. As soon as it became clear that we were serious, we agreed that while we didn't have to decide on the time line and method just then, we both wanted to be parents. When we became aunts to our two nephews, we got a preview of the experience of having kids in our lives: exhausting, messy, but funny and magical and something we definitely wanted.

So in that room, when I said to my soon-to-be wife, "I don't know if I want to have children," I felt surprise, and then that pre-cry tingle in my sinuses. I repeated myself, hardly believing what was coming out of my mouth. "I don't know if I want children." I felt like I was going to start crying, and then I didn't. I just sat there with the knowledge, knowledge that felt new even though it wasn't at all.

In my lifetime, my feelings about motherhood run the spectrum from ambivalent to eager. I love babies, their chubby legs and concerned faces and pugilist's fists; I am actively distressed by toddlers, their lack of reason, their id-ness, their sociopathy; I love older children who can talk about school and the books they're reading; and teenagers remain an utterly unknown—and intimidating—horizon. A hypochondriac, I am terrified of pregnancy and its medical risks. A hedonist, I don't want to give up whiskey cocktails, sushi, soft cheeses. A writer, I'm scared to relinquish writing time for child-rearing.

When I was younger, I didn't know if I wanted kids. Then, the first time I fell in love, at the tender age of twenty-three, a kind of hormonal switch flipped, and I went from uncertainty to cramping with want. I thought about having babies with an uncanny focus, even when I wasn't dating anybody, even when I didn't want to be pregnant. I had dream after dream about being pregnant. They were always the same: lying on my bed running my hand over a swollen belly, knowing that soon everything would change.

When I was a child, my love for my mother was uncomplicated. I was sick a lot, and because she didn't work outside the home, she spent a lot of time ferrying me to doctors. When I was home, I'd watch soap operas with her—she loved *All My Children*—while she ironed or did aerobics. I think she adored this version of me, whose difficulties were, for all intents and purposes, childlike. She was a good mother for young children.

My mom was one of nine kids—nine kids on a farm who never had anything of their own. She struggled with school but had a scrappy can-do attitude that took her to Florida when she was eighteen, far away from her native Wisconsin. She could be so funny and charming and kind. But her side of the family has always been marked with difficult personalities: stubbornness and self-righteousness. Traits that I, woefully, inherited.

The older I got, the more complicated our relationship became. Every teen's mother doesn't get them, but it seemed—to me—that my mother didn't get me *the most*. I was older and more complicated and my problems were older and more complicated.

I didn't need my mother, specifically, as much; I needed a complicated network of things: mental health support and a chemistry tutor and a job and a world that didn't shame fat teens or hate women and a queer mentor and someone to help me apply for college and the recession to not start the same year I graduated. My siblings, too, began to grow into more mature and difficult versions of themselves, and we exited her orbit.

My mom decided she wanted to go back to college to get her associate degree, which she did. After that, she bounced from job to job, trying to find her passion: real estate, special education, furniture restoration, retail. Nothing ever really stuck. As her frustration with her life mounted, I flourished in school, went to college, got my MFA. A vast and unbridgeable crevasse erupted between us. Whenever I saw her, she found some way to let me know that despite my accomplishments, I was failing. "You need to learn to make better choices," she told me, though what choices they were, she never specified. Besides, all I could hear was, *I wish I'd made better choices.* And I couldn't help her with that.

In the couple of months following graduate school, I moved home to southeastern Pennsylvania. Val and I—then girlfriends— were both job hunting from our respective parents' houses, but her parents were much happier to have her. My own had several hissing fights about my presence: my father insisted that I was welcome any time, because they were my parents and they loved me, and my mother told me it was *not* my house, and she was only letting me stay because my father insisted. I know it's not my house, I told her. As soon as Val and I got jobs and a place in Philadelphia, we'd be gone.

I slept in an uncomfortable guest room, my brother's former room, which was crammed with so much furniture there was nowhere to store a suitcase or walk. My mother forbade me from eating and drinking in there, because I might "make a mess." She would open the bedroom door periodically to "check" on things, to make sure—I don't know, that I wasn't doing a blood sacrifice or taking up beekeeping in her guest room? If the bedsheets were flipped down or my pajamas were lying across the bedspread, I'd hear a bloodcurdling yell that moved around the house like a bird. The stereotype of Midwestern passive-aggressiveness has never really suited my mother; she needs to say something about everything, needs to fight. It's something I've inherited from her, actually. It's one of my worst, and best, traits.

During the day, I hunted for jobs in Philadelphia and did freelance writing. The house was crowded with sounds (the news at full volume, my mom yelling at my father), so I sat on the back porch and worked, listening to the birds and the distant *thunk* of soccer balls. Periodically, my mother would come outside and look at me. "You can't just sit there," she said. "You have to find a job."

"I'm working," I'd say, and gesture to my computer.

"What was the point of all of that fancy graduate school," she asked, "if you can't find a job?"

It was such an odd question because it both saw to the heart

of my anxiety—what *was* I going to do post–graduate school?—
and also reflected how little she knew or understood about
me and my life. I tried to explain the work to her—I was earn-
ing $35 an hour just "sitting there," and why would I apply for
jobs here when I was moving to Philadelphia?—but she didn't
seem to believe or understand me, as if work was one singular
thing, and if I wasn't folding clothes or pushing a broom in my
hometown, I wasn't truly working. She circled arbitrary jobs in
the wanted ads from the local paper—did I want to be a school
bus driver? A telemarketer? What about data entry?—and left
them next to me. I got very good at theatrically chucking the
newsprint into the trash can.

"How are you going to pay back those student loans if you
don't get a job?" she asked.

"I've never missed a payment," I said. "And I *have* a job."

"You're never going to pay back those student loans, and then,
you know, your father and I are on the hook for them. Did you
know that?"

And around and around we went. A reader might think
that this is, obviously, a kind of misplaced parental anxiety and
love. And they might be right. But I felt like I was losing my
mind. There was no trust, no affection, no *listening*, just ignorant micromanagement. It felt like I was existing in a parallel
universe where everything I'd just done with my life, everything
I was doing with my life, hadn't made any difference at all. I was
a kid again, useless. Nothing was mine—not my time, not my

schedule, not my choices. (*If you oversleep, you won't get a job / if you go visit your girlfriend too much, you won't get a job / did you know you need a job to pay back your student loans / why did you go to school if you can't get a job to pay back your student loans. . . .)*

"Don't think you can just stay here," she said to me one afternoon. "Don't think you can just move in here and live in this house."

"If you think *for one second,*" I said, "that I want to stay in this demented, hellish, Kinkadian nightmare of a house with you breathing down my neck, instead of living in Philadelphia with my girlfriend, you are really and truly insane."

She set her jaw hard and didn't say anything. I couldn't tell what she wanted from me, except to get as far away from her as humanly possible. So I did.

Toward the end of my time at my parents' house, Val visited me. She was making headway on the job hunt, and we missed each other. Not wanting to deal with my mother, we sat up in my room, drinking seltzer water and eating popcorn and watching a movie on my laptop. Downstairs, my mother caught wind of the indiscretion, the breaking of her no-food-and-drink rule—the smell of popcorn, maybe, or that parental sixth sense—and she started to scream. Her voice wafted up the stairs, reedy and enraging. I heard her talking to my father, in the way that she always did when I was a kid—a harsh conversation meant to be overheard, to induce shame. I was ungrateful, she said. I was useless and disrespectful. I didn't belong here and she wanted me to leave.

Something inside of me popped, the way it does when you throw out your back. I was, I realized, up against an immovable, illogical object, and I might as well lose my shit because being reasonable and thoughtful wasn't going to get me anywhere. I came downstairs with the popcorn and stood in front of my mother.

"You are a nightmare," I told her. "You're ignorant and bitter and you and this house are a living nightmare. You're a miserable human being, and that is your right, but I refuse to be miserable with you."

"You're selfish," she said. "You're selfish and stuck-up and you think everything belongs to you."

"Yup," I said, and very calmly poured the popcorn on the floor.

She got up and left the room. After she was gone, I scooped linty popcorn off the carpet and then dumped it all in the trash, then went upstairs and went to bed. The next morning, Val and I drove to Philadelphia and stayed at a friend's apartment. We moved there a few weeks later; Val got a full-time job, and I pieced together part-time jobs: adjuncting, retail, freelancing. We made it work; it has worked ever since.

But I relished that moment—that moment in which I'd finally made the mess she always thought I'd make. It was satisfying, in its own way, to fulfill her expectations so neatly, knowing I'd never have to do it again.

. . .

My mother and I do not speak anymore. It didn't start at that moment, with the popcorn, but that was the beginning of something—a realization that I had choices about how to live my life, and one of them was her not being in it. It's been five years, now. She didn't come to my wedding—I had to "repair our relationship" before she would deign to attend, she said over email, and I never even bothered replying. The word, I guess, is "estranged," and there is indeed something strange about it: I think of her distantly, like someone I knew from an intro-to-biology class my first semester in college, instead of the woman who raised me.

I don't know what she makes of me, now. Everything I am is proof that she was wrong about me, and yet the woman I've known for my entire life does not apologize, does not admit to fault. I believe that she loves me, in the same way that I believe that it's best that we are not a part of each other's lives. Because my identity has been shaped by what she is not; she is, for me, an example of how not to conduct a life. I believe that her pride in my accomplishments—and her love for me—is actively battling her resentment, but I don't want to oversee that civil war, and I don't have to.

So, parenthood. I am stopped short by any number of concerns, ranging from practical ones—the cost—to selfish ones—my wife's and my careers and our enjoyment of each other—to illogical ones—the idea that my one-day child might grow up and write an essay about me in an anthology called *What My Mother and I Don't Talk About II*, and I might only then have a clear, bird's-eye view of my own faults and foibles.

I think my mom wanted to live a selfish existence. I do not think she imagined herself struggling to find her identity in her forties, fifties, sixties. And I don't blame her. I want to be selfish, too. I want to write books and travel and sleep in late. I want to cook weird, complicated meals and have unadulterated time with my wife. The difference between us—besides the fact that she made her choice, and I have yet to make mine—is that with my wife, the act of making a baby is by definition purposeful. We have to save money, pick sperm, go through complicated and expensive and invasive procedures to become parents. We cannot accidentally stumble into parenthood the way straight couples do. And it's better that way, I think. No *oops*, followed by a lifelong hydra of anger that cannot be managed or maintained. But of course this is the kind of problem where you can't learn from one way and choose another. You're a parent, or you're not.

This is what my mother and I don't talk about: That it is not my fault she is so profoundly unhappy with her life. That she had a chance to know me—really know me, as an adult and an artist and a human being—and she blew it. That I have not regretted our estrangement for one single second; in fact, I keep waiting for the regret to appear and being surprised when it doesn't. That I feel bad for her that she is so dissatisfied with her own life; I wouldn't wish that on my worst enemy. That I miss what we had when I was a kid, but I'm not a kid anymore, and I will never be again. And that the thing that keeps me from tackling parenthood with eagerness is not, really, money or ambition or hypochondria or selfishness. Rather, it's the fear that I've learned less from my childhood than I should have, that I am more like her than I want to be.

Are You Listening?

By André Aciman

I always knew my mother couldn't hear, but I can't remember when it dawned on me that she'd always be deaf. If I was told, I didn't believe it. It was no different when I learned about sex. Someone may have sat me down for the facts of life, and although I wasn't really shocked and probably already knew, I couldn't bring myself to trust any of it. In between knowing something and refusing to know it lies a murky chasm that even the most enlightened among us are perfectly happy to inhabit. If anyone gave me the official report on my mother, it would have been my grandmother, who did not like her daughter-in-law and who found my mother's deaf friends as repellent as ungainly fowls squawking in her son's living room. If it wasn't my grandmother, it would have been the way people made fun of my mother on the street.

Some men whistled when she walked by, because she was beautiful and sexy and had a way of looking you boldly in the face until you lowered your eyes. But when she shopped and spoke with the monotonous, guttural voice of the deaf, people laughed. In Alexandria, Egypt, where we lived until we were summarily exiled, like all of the country's Jews, that's what you did when someone was different. It wasn't full-throated laughter; it was derision, the stepchild of contempt, which is as mirthless as it is cruel. She couldn't hear their laughter, but she read it in their faces. This must be how she finally understood why people always smirked when she thought she was speaking like everyone else. Who knows how long it took her to realize that she was unlike other children, why some turned away, or others, meaning to be kind, had a diffident way when they allowed her to play with them?

Born in Alexandria in 1924 in the wake of British colonial rule, my mother belonged to a middle-class, French-speaking Jewish family. Her father had done well as a bicycle merchant and spared no expense to find a cure for her deafness. Her mother took her to see the most prominent audiologists in Europe but returned more disheartened after each appointment. There was, the doctors said, no cure. Her child had lost her hearing to meningitis when she was a few months old, and from meningitis there was no coming back. Her ears were healthy, but meningitis had touched the part of her brain responsible for hearing.

In those days, there was nothing resembling deaf pride. Deafness was a stigma. The very poor often neglected their deaf children, condemning them to a lifetime of menial labor. Children remained illiterate, and their language was primitive, gestural. In the snobbish view of my mother's parents, if you couldn't cure deafness, you learned to hide it. If you weren't ashamed of it, you were taught to be. You learned how to lip-read, not sign; you learned to speak with your voice, not your hands. You didn't eat with your hands; why on earth would you speak with them?

My mother was initially enrolled in a Jewish French day school, but within weeks her parents and the teachers realized that the school couldn't accommodate a deaf child, so she was shipped off to a specialized school in Paris, overseen by nuns. It turned out to be more of a finishing school than a school for the deaf. She was taught good posture by walking with a book on her head and by holding books between her elbows and her waist when she sat at a dinner table. She picked up sewing, knitting, and needlepoint. But she was a volatile, rambunctious child and had grown into a tomboy who collected bicycles from her father's shop. She didn't like to play with dolls. She had no patience for French savoir faire or for French grace and deportment.

She came back to Alexandria two years later, where she was turned over to a well-intentioned and innovative Greek woman who ran a French private school for the deaf in her villa. The school was welcoming and forgiving, and vibrated with a sense of its mission. Classwork, however, consisted of long, grueling hours learning how to mimic sounds that my mother would never be able to hear. The rest of the time was devoted to lipreading sessions: frontal lipreading and, in my mother's case, because she was a quick learner, profile lipreading. She learned how to read and write, acquired a rudimentary knowledge of sign language, was taught history and some literature, and at graduation was awarded a French bronze medal by a general who happened to be passing through Alexandria.

Still, she had spent her first eighteen years learning how to do what couldn't have seemed more unnatural: pretending to hear. It was no better than teaching a blind person to count his steps from this pillar to that post so as not to be caught with a white stick. She learned to laugh at a joke even if she would have needed to hear the play on words in the punch line. She nodded at precisely the right intervals to someone speaking to her in Russian, to the point where the Russian was convinced that she understood everything he'd been saying.

The Greek headmistress was idolized by her students, but her method had disastrous consequences for my mother's ability to process and synthesize complex ideas. Past a certain threshold, things simply stopped making sense to her. She could talk politics if you outlined the promises made by a presidential candidate, but she was unable to think through the inconsistencies in his agenda, even when they were explained to her. She lacked the conceptual framework or the symbolic sophistication to acquire and use an abstract vocabulary. She might like a painting by Monet, but she couldn't discuss the beauty of a poem by Baudelaire.

When I asked her a question such as "Can God create a stone too heavy for Him to lift?" or "Is the Cretan lying when he says that all Cretans are liars?" she did not understand it. Did she think in words? I'd ask. She did not know. If not in words, how did she organize her thoughts? She did not know that, either. Does anyone? Asked when she realized she was deaf, or what life was like without hearing, or whether she minded not hearing Bach or Beethoven, she'd say she hadn't really thought about it. You might as well have asked a blind person to describe colors. Wit, too, eluded her, though she loved comedy, jesting, and slapstick. She was an accomplished mimic and was drawn to the voiceless Harpo Marx, whose jokes were rooted not in speech but in body language.

She had a circle of devoted deaf friends, but unlike a deaf person today, who might be able to finger spell every word in the *Oxford English Dictionary*, they used a language without an alphabet, just a shorthand lingo of hand and facial signs whose vocabulary seldom exceeded five hundred words. Her friends could discuss sewing, recipes, horoscopes. They could tell you they loved you, and they could be unsparingly kind with children and old people when they touched them, because hands speak more intimately than words. But intimacy is one thing, and complex ideas quite another.

After leaving school, my mother volunteered as a nurse in Alexandria. She drew blood, gave injections, and eventually served in a hospital, caring for wounded British soldiers during the Second World War. She dated a few of them and would take them out for a spin on the motorbike that her father had given her on her eighteenth birthday. She liked to go to parties and had a surprising gift for fast dancing. She became a coveted partner for anyone who wanted to jitterbug or go for an early morning swim at the beach.

When my father met her, she wasn't yet twenty. He was stunned by her beauty, her warmth, her unusual mixture of meekness and in-your-face boldness. That was how she compensated for being deaf, and it sometimes made you forget that she was. She charmed his friends and his family, except for his parents. Her future father-in-law called her "the cripple," his wife "a gold digger." But my father refused to listen to them, and three years later they were married. In her wedding pictures, she is beaming. Her Greek teacher applauded her triumph: she had married out of the deaf ghetto.

Now I can see that with a better education she might have become someone else. Her intelligence and her combative perseverance in the face of so many obstacles in Egypt as a Jew—and, after Egypt, in Italy and then the US—would have made her a great career woman. She might have become a physician or a psychiatrist. In a less enlightened age, she remained a housewife. Even though she was well-off, she was not only a woman but a deaf woman. Two strikes.

She spoke and understood French, learned Greek and basic Arabic, and when we landed in Italy, she picked up Italian by going to the market every day. When she didn't understand something, she pretended that she did until she got it. She almost always got it. In the consulate in Naples, weeks before immigrating to the United States, in 1968, she had her first encounter with American English. She was asked to raise her right hand and repeat the oath of allegiance. She babbled some soft-spoken sounds that the American functionary was happy to mistake for the oath. The scene was so awkward that it brought out nervous giggles in my brother and me. My mother laughed with us as we walked out of the building, but my father had to be told why it was funny.

Her deafness had always stood like an insuperable wall between them, and the longer they stayed married the more difficult it was to scale. In retrospect, it had always stood there. My father loved classical music; she had never been to a concert. He read long Russian novels and modern French writers whose prose was cadenced and brilliant. She preferred fashion magazines. He liked to stay at home and read after work; she liked to go dancing and have friends over for dinner. She had grown up enjoying American movies, because in Egypt they had French subtitles; he preferred French films, which had no subtitles and were therefore lost on her, because lip-reading actors on the screen proved almost impossible. His friends spoke about the most rarefied things imaginable: the Greco-Egyptian god Serapis, the archeological digs around Alexandria, the novels of Curzio Malaparte; she loved gossip.

Not long after they were married, they both realized how

utterly unsuited they were. They loved each other until the very end, but they misunderstood and insulted each other, and quarreled every day. He often went out when her deaf friends visited. In the 1960s, he left home altogether for a few years, coming back just weeks before we were to leave Egypt. Those of her friends who married out of the deaf community had tumultuous marriages, too. Only those who stayed with the deaf seemed to find as much happiness as the hearing.

My mother never really did learn English. Lip movements were not clear or declarative enough, unless you seemed to parody what you were saying for comic effect. She didn't like it when I exaggerated my lip movements to her in public, because they proclaimed her deafness. Many pitied her, and some made an effort to cross the barrier. Some well-meaning people tried to communicate with her by mimicking the speech of the deaf, aping a raucous voice and making distorted faces. Others spoke loudly, as though raising the decibel level might get their point across. She could tell they were yelling. Then there were those who, try as they might, were never able to understand what my mother was saying to them, and those who didn't care to make the effort. They refused to look her in the face or even to acknowledge her presence at the dining table.

Or people just laughed.

When friends at the playground asked why my mother spoke with that strange voice, I would say, "Because that is how she speaks." Her voice didn't sound strange until it was pointed out to me. It was Mom's voice—the voice that woke me up in the morning, that called out to me at the beach, that soothed me and told me tales at bedtime.

Sometimes I tried to persuade myself that she was not really deaf. She was a mischievous prankster, and what better way to keep everyone hopping than to pretend she was deaf, the way every child has, at one point or another, pretended to be blind or played dead? For some reason, she had forgotten to stop playing her prank. To test her, I would slide behind her when she wasn't looking and yell in her ear. No response. Not a shudder. What amazing control she had. I sometimes ran to her and said that someone was ringing the doorbell. She opened the door; then, realizing I had played a low trick on her, she would laugh it off, because wasn't it funny how the joy of her life—me—had hatched this practical joke to remind her, like everyone else, that she was deaf? One day, I watched her get dressed up to go out with my father and, as she was fastening a pair of earrings, I told her she was beautiful. Yes, I am beautiful. But it doesn't change anything. I am still deaf—meaning, and don't you forget it.

It was difficult for a child to reconcile her ready smile, her love of comedy and good fellowship with her enduring grief as a wife and a deaf person. She always cried with her friends. They all cried. But those of us who have lived with the deaf stop feeling sorry for them. Instead, one jumps quickly from pity to cruelty, like a pebble skittering on shallow water, without understanding what it means to live without sound. I seldom have been able to sit still and force myself to feel her seclusion. It was much easier to lose my temper when she wouldn't listen, because she never listened—because part of understanding what you said seemed to involve a mixture of guesswork and intuition, where the shading of facts meant more than the facts themselves.

Nothing was a greater ordeal than making phone calls for my mother. She often asked my brother or me to help her, dialing the number and speaking for her as she stood there, watching every word. She appreciated it and was proud that at so young an age we were able to call the plumber, her friends, her seamstress. She told me that I was her ears. "He is her ears," her mother-in-law would proclaim. She meant, Thank the good Lord there was someone to do her dirty work for her. Otherwise, how could that poor woman survive?

There were two ways to get out of making phone calls. One was to hide. The other was to lie. I would dial the number, wait awhile, and then tell her that the line was busy. Five minutes later, the line was still busy. It never occurred to me that the call might be urgent or, when her husband failed to show up for dinner, that she was desperate to talk to a friend or a relative, anyone to shield her from her loneliness. Sometimes men called, but, with my brother and me as go-betweens, the conversations were awkward. The men never called again.

When I went to graduate school, it fell to my brother to stand by as a middleman. I would speak to him, he would relay the message, and in the background I would make out her voice telling him what to say, which he would relay back to me. Sometimes I would ask him to put her on the phone and let her tell me whatever came to mind, because I missed her voice and wanted to hear her say the things she had always said to me, slurring her words a bit, ungrammatical, words that weren't necessarily words even, just sounds that reached far back to my childhood, when I didn't know words.

As a child, I had fantasized that someday someone would invent a gizmo that would allow my mother to telephone another deaf person. The miracle occurred about thirty years ago, when I obtained a teletypewriter for her. For the first time in her life, she was able to communicate with her deaf friends without involving me or my brother. She could type long messages in broken English and arrange to see them. Then, seven years ago, I installed a device on her TV that allowed her to communicate visually with friends around the country. Most were too old to travel, so this was a godsend.

Open to any new experience, she fell in love with each technological advance. (My father, ever reluctant to approach anything new, remained attached to his shortwave radio.) Several years ago, when my mother was in her mideighties, I bought her an iPad, so that she could Skype and FaceTime for hours with friends abroad, people she hadn't seen in ages. It was better than anything I had imagined as a boy. She could call me when I was at home, at the office, at the gym, even at Starbucks. I could FaceTime with her and not worry where she was or how she was doing. After my father died, she insisted on living alone, and my biggest fear was that she would fall and hurt herself. FaceTime also meant that I was spared having to visit her so often, as she well understood: "Does this mean that you're not coming over tonight because we're speaking with my iPad?"

My mother, for all her deficits, was among the most sagacious people I have known. Language was a prosthesis, a grafted limb that she had learned to live with but that remained peripheral because she could do without it. She had more immediate ways of communicating. She was acutely discerning and had a flair for people and situations—from the Latin verb *fragrare*, to scent. Her radar was always on: whom to trust, what to believe, and how to read an inflection. She made up in scent what she had lost in her deafness. She taught me spices, naming them in a grocery store by dipping her palm into the burlap bags and letting me sniff each handful. She taught me to recognize her perfumes, the smell of damp wool, the smell of leaking gas. When I write about scent, I am channeling not Proust but my mother.

People were often immediately drawn to her. You might attribute this to the expansive good cheer she radiated whenever she went out. But my mother was a profoundly unhappy soul. I think it was her unhindered capacity to let intimacy happen at a glance, with everyone—rich, poor, good, bad, butcher, postman, grandee, or Senegalese workers at supermarkets on the Upper West Side who helped her without knowing that she, too, was a native French speaker. If she had been dropped into Kandahar or Islamabad, she would have had no trouble finding the cut of beef she wanted and haggling over the price until she prevailed, while making friends with others in the marketplace.

She made you want to offer intimacy, too. Better yet, she made you reach into yourself to find it, in case you'd mislaid it or never knew you had it in you to give. This was her language, and as with prisoners in separate cells learning to tap a new language with its own peculiar grammar and alphabet, she taught you to speak it. Sometimes my friends, within an hour of meeting her, forgot that she couldn't hear them and came to understand everything she said, even when they couldn't understand a word of French, much less French spoken by a deaf person. I'd try to step in and interpret for them. "I get it," my friend would say. "I understand perfectly," my mother would say—meaning, Leave us alone and stop meddling; we're doing just fine. I was the one not understanding.

One day a few years ago, I stopped by my mother's apartment during a jog on a very cold day, to warm up and catch my breath and see how she was doing. She had been watching TV. I sat next to her and explained that I wasn't able to come to dinner that night because I was going out with friends, but that I might drop in the next day for our ritual scotch and dinner. She liked that. What did I want her to cook? I suggested her baked ziti, with the top slightly crisp. She thought it was a great idea. I had forgotten to remove my ski mask, and the entire conversation took place with my lips covered. She was listening to me by following the movement of my eyebrows.

In the New World where my mother ended her days, you got respect and had equal rights; you thrived with dignity and security. She liked it better than the Old World. But it wasn't her home. Now that I think of what Shakespeare might have called her "unaccommodated" language, I realize how much I miss its immediate, tactile quality from another age, when your face was your bond, not your words. I owe this language not to the books I read or studied but to my mother, who had no faith in, and no talent or much patience for, words.

Brother, Can You Spare Some Change?

By Sari Botton

"Would you like this top?" My mother holds out an animal-print blouse with the price tag still on. It's something I wouldn't be caught dead in and she likely knows it, but still she's eager for me to take it, to receive it from her. "I just bought it," she says, "but maybe it would be better on you."

"No, thank you, Mom," I say, trying to hide my annoyance and discomfort—feeling more like thirteen than twenty-three, and a year out of college.

"I have another shirt you might like," she says, returning to her closet. She comes back with a navy cotton Michael Stars French-cut long-sleeve tee, one I've borrowed from her at least once before, now dusty with the powder her dermatologist prescribes. "This is more you." It is.

"But it's *your* shirt," I protest.

"I can get another one," she insists. "I'll go back to Blooming-dale's. Or do you want to go with me? I can get you a new one there—I want to get you something."

I'm afraid it would hurt her if I share with her that a part of me is reluctant to trust her gifts. I worry there are strings at-tached. More than that, it all feels like a betrayal of everything she'd trained me to believe in and to be. Deep down, I'm also afraid that if I speak up, the giving will stop.

Five years earlier, the summer after my first year at college, I became a thief.

A few times a week, I crept into my annoying one-year-older stepbrother Jared's room, dipped into his huge fishbowl brim-ming with grimy nickels, dimes, and quarters, and snuck off with seventy-five cents, maybe a dollar.

I didn't think of it as stealing. That wouldn't jibe with my long-established, uncontested role as The Good Daughter. I told myself I was borrowing my stepbrother's money—even though I hadn't ever asked. Also: I never made any effort to repay it.

Sometimes, instead of a loan, I thought of it as war repara-tions. On the outwardly civil but quietly vicious battlefield of my parents' divorce, I had been the clear loser. I was saddled with two parents who, in their new marriages, were the partners with the least money, the least power, the least balls to stand up for their own kids.

When I was twelve, my father got remarried to a widow

whose late husband endowed her and her two daughters with healthy trust funds. Each year, their grandmother, a sort of Semitic Boston Brahmin, would proudly hand me a Chanukah card, inside of which she'd tucked one newly minted, crisp dollar bill.

When I was fifteen, my mother met a widower who let her know early on he'd prefer not to marry a woman with kids. My mother did a decent impression of a childless woman in a variety of ways. When she bought things for my sister and me, she would take us aside and whisper, "Go look under your bed—I left something there for you," so my stepfather wouldn't know.

And so, at eighteen, putting myself through school, I felt sorry for myself, and as consolation, awarded myself a small amount of financial aid from my stepbrother's bountiful change collection. What was the chance he'd notice a few coins missing here and there, anyway?

I was skimming the change for the M32 bus, which I rode each workday from Penn Station to the Book of the Month Club, where I had a summer job that would help me pay for my next semester—fall 1984. I traveled into the city on the 6:47 a.m. from Oceanside, Long Island, and back on the 5:43 p.m. with my mother's husband, Bernard, a miserable human being, *a farbissener*, my grandmother said. Every morning I was confronted by his ulcer breath and beady eyes, magnified behind thick, intense prescription Porsche aviators, at an hour when I found it hard to focus at all, let alone smile—a complaint he lodged against me with my mother. It was obvious, though, that Bernard wasn't happy about having to share his ride with me either. There was a tension about his silence. Not only didn't I want to talk to him, I was afraid to. He had a temper. I worried that anything I said might make him erupt, and so on those rides, I mostly pretended to sleep.

This is the terminology we used when we referred to Bernard: "He has a temper." That's what we called it when he threw a glass serving bowl filled with spaghetti at his son's head, giving him a concussion; when he threw a wineglass at my mother and it shattered on the floor after bouncing off the side of her face. That's what we called it when he dragged my thirteen-year-old sister down the stairs by her hair, when he gripped his hands around her throat and violently shook her, leaving marks. That's what we called it when we sought refuge at my mother's friend's house. When my mother went back, begging Bernard's forgiveness for leaving. When someone—probably my mother's friend—anonymously called Child Protective Services, and a social worker started paying visits to our house.

He has a temper.

That's what we called it when he threw my ceramic piggy bank at me one evening while I was sitting on my bed, doing my high school homework. He burst into my room waving a legal pad with numbers scratched in pencil, fuming that I wasn't willing to call my father and ask him to pay more in child support. I ducked just in time. The piggy bank hit the wall and smashed to pieces.

· · ·

All summer I got away with my petty thievery. As I went along, I became cavalier, and concerned myself less and less with any injustice associated with it. I got so comfortable it became perfectly routine.

At the end of August, though, I was in for a surprise. It turned out my stepbrother kept a close accounting of the change in that bowl. On a Saturday night the week before we were each headed upstate to our respective colleges for sophomore year, he came down to dinner livid, practically foaming at the mouth. He pointed the finger . . . at my sister.

"*She* took it," he shouted. "I know she did!"

"No I didn't!" she shrieked.

"Well, then who did, huh?"

I sat there, stunned, saying nothing. My sister and stepbrother continued their shouting match into the night. My sister cried as she pleaded with my mother to believe her.

Before I even considered fessing up, I gave thought to whether it was plausible to suggest someone else might have taken the money. Was there some phantom I could pin this on to make it go away? Someone who might have come to visit? But then I heard my stepbrother insist it had to have been my sister or someone else in the house because he'd been tracking the steady shrinkage over the past two months.

I don't think I've ever felt worse than I did for the twelve hours I let my sister wrongly take the blame. I had to come clean, but I barely knew how. Confessing to crimes wasn't in my vocabulary. Whenever my sister got caught misbehaving, after a little kicking and screaming it never took her long to admit she was wrong and take her lumps. The idea of that was foreign and frightening to me. I was so well rehearsed at playing the angel. I dreaded the thought of having my perfect image tarnished. *Who am I without my halo?*

That entire night I sat up writing and rewriting confession notes on the colored personalized stationery I had received as a bat mitzvah present. At five a.m., I placed them in envelopes and left one at each person's regular seat at the Formica breakfast nook. I included a check in my stepbrother's.

Later, I hid in my room, wincing as I listened to the conversation downstairs after it was clear the letters had been opened. I heard my sister hiss, "See?!" I heard my stepbrother say, "Yeah, you probably stole some too." I heard her laugh in his face.

After a while, my mom came upstairs. *"You?"* she asked. She hardly knew what else to say.

Driving my mother's transformation was her recent marriage, her third—in every possible way, Stanley, my mother's third husband, was unlike Bernard. Stanley was warm, kind, lighthearted—a balding amateur magician who called himself "The Great Baldini." Stanley was thoughtful and ceaselessly generous.

While Stanley wasn't quite *rich*, he was much better off than my mother's first two husbands (including my dad), which meant he had more to share. But for much of my life I'd been brushing up against people with money—relatives, family friends, step-relatives with trust funds—and most of them kept it all to themselves. Stanley was different: a gem, a mensch. From the first week he met us, he treated my sister and me as if we were his own, taking us out to nice restaurants, showering us with birthday and Chanukah gifts, and later, helping me out when I was broke.

In this new marriage, my mother was a different person. The woman I'd known in the midseventies as a struggling single mom barely making ends meet on an elementary school teacher's salary—a socialist "pinko," as some friends joked, a head of the local NYSUT chapter, who drove a beat-up Dodge Dart—that woman was now unrecognizable to me.

Now she went for weekly manicures and pedicures, and had weekly cleaning help instead of just once in a while. A whole new category of apparel sprung up in her walk-in closet—sparkly evening wear for the dinner dances and cocktail parties she often attended on Stanley's arm. She received gifts of gold jewelry for special occasions and went on vacations to tropical places.

As part of the transition, my mother also suddenly became much more generous toward her daughters. In her marriage to Bernard, giving to us had been difficult for her, in large part because she was afraid of setting off Bernard's temper. It was a strategic choice, a way of managing the angriest person in the room.

Once Bernard was gone and Stanley was in the picture, my mother was reborn. Now when I visited, there was The Ritual Offering of Things. By the end of a weekend visit, I'd be weighed down with all manner of apparel, shoes, tchotchkes, food, and Clinique samples that came with the lipstick she'd just bought at Bloomingdale's.

She'd offer to take me shopping there and I'd recoil. Yet at thirteen, in the aftermath of my parents' divorce, I'd wished for this. I would beg my mother to take us to Bloomingdale's the way other kids beg their parents to take them to Disney. Shopping (or more accurately, *browsing*) there helped me safeguard against feeling as if we were impoverished products of divorce, which we now absolutely were. After my parents split up, I became very concerned about my outward appearance and became painfully status conscious. I was determined not to look or feel like some sort of disheveled urchin, like some other divorce kids I knew—always in scuffed shoes and clothes they'd outgrown, with dirty, matted hair. Somehow just being inside Bloomingdale's had the power to temporarily quell my anxiety about this.

For a short time in the aisles there, I could see something resembling *want* peeking through my mother's antimaterialism pose. We had a ritual: First, the three of us would share two soups and one salad in the store's restaurant, called Ondine. Once we were fueled up, we'd hit the Clinique counter. Next we were off to the girls' department, and finally the ladies' department, where we'd advise my mother on which of the outfits she wasn't going to buy looked best on her.

We never bought clothes—just tried them on. But at the end of each outing, we'd head to the gourmet food department in the basement where my mother would pick up a small jar of Tiptree Little Scarlet preserves, crammed with countless perfect, tiny strawberries peeking out from the glass, and treat us each to a mini Godiva chocolate bar.

At twenty-three, the conspicuous consumption and giving made me terribly uncomfortable. Who was this bougie lady, and what had she done with my mother, the prole? Where was the woman who, in the summer of 1976, had broken up with my father, even though without him, she'd have to face an even greater financial struggle than the ongoing one she'd been accustomed to?

The Bloomingdale's browsing outings, and pretty much anything else enjoyable, came to an end when Bernard and his two sons entered our lives in early 1981, when I was fifteen. The next six years were bleak and somber, and polluted with rage, ours suppressed, Bernard's randomly exploded into moments of unforgettable violence.

After one of Bernard's outbursts—when he threw my sister's three-in-one stereo at her, and later dragged her down the stairs by her hair—my mother filed divorce papers. It was a relief when he moved out. I had no idea how much bigger a relief was ahead of us, just a few months later, when my mother started going out with Stanley.

. . .

Within a short amount of time after my mother and Stanley married, I stopped resisting and lapped up everything my mother offered, although always with some degree of reservation. Most of the time I protest a bit, and then acquiesce, accepting her offerings—for her benefit and for mine. I recognize now that she needs to give to me as desperately as I had once needed her to.

She isn't just giving me things. She's giving me *giving*, something she hadn't been able to do for so long, which she regretted. In receiving, I give to her the satisfaction of *having given*.

In May of 2018, at eighty-nine, Stanley suddenly became severely ill. Within a few weeks, a month shy of their thirtieth anniversary, he was gone. My mother's whole world and her financial stability began crumbling.

In the week after the funeral, I go to help her pack up the winter apartment in Boca Raton. She needs more of the Clinique hypoallergenic foundation she still uses, and asks if we can take a ride to Bloomingdale's for it.

It is strange being at a Bloomingdale's branch after so many years of almost never shopping in department stores. So much is exactly the same—the soft lighting, the chic interior design, the appealing merchandising. Some part of me gets a kind of high off the feeling of abundance in the air. I can tell my mother does too. There's a spring in her step I haven't seen since Stanley took ill.

• • •

"Do you need anything?" my mother asks.

"I'm fine," I say.

She stops to try on shoes on her way to the Clinique counter. As she slips her foot into a pair of FitFlop flats, she confesses that when Stanley had been in the ICU, she'd gone there to shop away her anxiety, and purchased two tops. Also, she slips in, she has over $600 worth of revolving debt on a Bloomingdale's charge card.

"Promise me that when the will is settled, you'll pay that off," I say. She promises.

These days, appropriately, the tables are turning. I'm fifty-three, she's seventy-eight, and it's my turn to take care of her. Fortunately she's got social security and a pension and other money, enough to cover her bills for now. I pick up the checks at dinner. I bring and send her little gifts—tickets to a local show; organic cranberry concentrate to mix with her seltzer; little pouches she collects to store makeup and jewelry; adult coloring books with positive aphorisms to help her through her grieving; chocolate-dipped macaroons. It feels good to be able to give back to her in what small ways I can.

I have no idea who my mother will become in this next phase of her life, and I can't help but worry she'll be vulnerable to the charms of another mean man like Bernard. I hope that no matter who comes along, though, my mother will rediscover her independence and the principles of nonmaterialism she taught me by example when I was a tween. They might have been a cover for her own rebellion and issues around self-worth, but they make a lot of sense to me now.

Her Body / My Body

By Nayomi Munaweera

I'm sitting on the toilet waiting for my mother. I have to wait for her because I am incapable of cleaning myself properly. As always, she keeps me waiting. When she comes, she makes disgusted faces as she wipes me. The message is that she doesn't want to do this but she *has to* because I am too stupid to do it right. There have been loud arguments about this issue. My father and my grandmother fighting with her to let me clean myself, saying it's not normal. She has defied them all; she is my mother and my body belongs to her.

I don't fight her. I believe her and know that I'm not capable of doing anything right. Only this time it's different—there's blood. I've gotten my first period. That's when my mother lets me start cleaning myself. That's when she lets me start showering without her overseeing. I am twelve years old.

The problem was that she saw no difference between her body and my body. I belonged to her completely. I was both her best, beloved precious child and a useless piece of shit. Sometimes she baked and made me dresses; other times she screamed that I was worthless. Constantly, I wavered between these two understandings of myself, never sure where to land, always looking for evidence as to what I was.

It had been easy when I was an infant. Then she had naturally controlled every aspect of my life, and this fed her need for subservience. It was later, when it became apparent that I would form a personality separate from hers, that I would not *be* her, that I had inherited traits from my father, whom she hated but whom she would not leave, that things got difficult. I remember hearing other adults talk about her rages. But they were afraid of getting involved in our internal family dynamics, and therefore no one intervened.

My parents often say that when I was a child, they could leave me alone in a room for hours. I would sit still and be quiet; I would not even move. They seem to see this as an indication that I was a good child, an obedient child. They don't see this as unusual behavior, masking deeper psychological implications.

Decades later, when I was in my thirties, living in San Francisco, and had found the therapist who would unlock all my life, I finally revealed how old I had been when my mother stopped treating me like an infant. I had never told anyone before. I imagined that if I told someone this shameful secret, they would realize that I was soiled and, therefore, inherently unlovable. I stuttered and wept and finally was able to say the words. He responded with these magic phrases: "It's not your fault. You didn't do anything wrong. You were just a child."

I left his office and wandered into a bookstore and from a second story overlooking Union Square I called my mother and asked her why she hadn't allowed me dominion over my own body. She said she couldn't remember but she had been young. Mostly she thought she was trying to do the best for me; she was trying to be a good mother. She was sad about it but there was nothing else to say. We never talked about it again.

The Wedding

My parents were married in 1972 in Sri Lanka. My mother was nineteen and the youngest child of a widow. When she was quite young, her father died of a stroke, and soon after, her eldest and favorite brother died in a violent car accident. She would never forget saying goodbye to her brother when she went to school in the morning and seeing his broken body brought to the house in the evening. In certain ways her heart was already split; she knew not to expect safety in the world.

My father was twenty-nine. He had just graduated as an engineer from the prestigious University of Peradeniya, one of the forty-eight engineers who had graduated in the entire island that year. He was very smart; he was very shy. He had been brought up by an intensely dominating mother who pushed him into success. In certain ways, his heart was already split; he knew not to expect too much joy in the world.

Their two formidable mothers had been little girls in the same village. They were "our people," so when the marriage proposal was brought, both families agreed. The man and girl knew each other a little. They might have gone to the movies a few times alone before they were married; anything more would have been unthinkable.

When I see their wedding picture, her, resplendent in a shining silver sari, him, so handsome in his black suit, both of them smiling, I am stunned by both awe and grief.

Immigrant Dreams

I was born exactly a year after. My mother always wanted more for us than Sri Lanka at the time could give, and so in 1976 when I was three, she convinced my father to immigrate to Nigeria. When a military coup happened in Nigeria in 1984, it was my mother who precipitated our move to the US. I was twelve and my sister, Namal, was three.

We were part of the first wave of Sri Lankan Americans, a tiny community of islanders in the suburbs of Los Angeles. If you saw us then, you would have seen the perfect immigrant family. You would have seen people who had pulled themselves up by their bootstraps.

Consider my father: In Nigeria he had been a respected

professional. In America his first job included rolling through raw sewage in flood control channels balanced on his stomach on a small wheeled board. From there he rose in the ranks of Los Angeles County until he was a very prominent engineer, an almost unbelievable life trajectory for a boy from a small Sri Lankan village.

Consider my mother: this girl who never went to college. In Nigeria she had been the principal of her own school. In California she started over as a preschool teacher. She opened the school at 6 a.m. and closed it at 6 p.m. and then she went home to cook and clean. Over two decades she saved up enough to buy a preschool and then another. She remade herself as a business owner, a homeowner.

In America, we knew we had to be very, very good. Americans often looked at us with suspicion. Sometimes they said we spoke English well and it was supposed to be a compliment. They didn't seem to know that we had been born with the language in our mouths because of a certain cruel history, so we smiled and said thank you. Other times they got angry and shouted that we should go home, and we knew that only perfection would convince them that we, too, were human.

We were tenacious, thrifty, and hardworking. Always we looked so good. My mother in a sari, my father in a suit with a tie that matched her sari, their two pretty daughters. How we glittered and dazzled at the immigrant parties that were the whole of our social life in that strange place, Sri Lanka in Los Angeles, Colombo meeting Hollywood. It was important to shine in this small community of two hundred families. Not doing so meant risking being ostracized, and who could survive in the wilds of America without the balm of one's own people?

Inside the House

My mother was the queen and we were her loyal subjects. Any assertion of individual identity was an indication of abandonment, a sign that we did not love her. When she thought that we did not love her, the queen disappeared and the witch arrived.

When we sensed her mood shifting toward darkness, we would whisper to each other, "Coming colors no good." This was shorthand to describe something unnamed and insidious. My mother screamed, she smashed dishes until there wasn't a single unbroken plate in the house, she said cruel things that lodged themselves in my brain and took decades to unhear. She broke the framed wedding pictures so many times that we stopped having them reframed. She locked herself in the bathroom and wept and wept. Sometimes she went silent for days. She could go from crying uncontrollably to laughing in minutes. If we were still spinning in the aftermath of her hurricane, she would ask us what was wrong. If we didn't mirror her jubilance, the anger would return. So we learned to ignore our own feelings until we didn't feel them anymore.

I'm fourteen and my mother has been raging for hours. My father, my sister, and I have been watching TV, either *Gilligan's*

Island or *The Three Stooges*, our favorite shows then and an easy way to anesthetize. Now it is suspiciously quiet so I go to check. She's in the bathroom, a long deep slash across her wrist. There's blood in the sink, on the wall. She's dazed, incoherent, babbling. I wash the blood off her wrists, bind the wound tightly with bandages we keep in the cabinet. I ask her why, but she doesn't answer. I put her to bed. I never talk to my dad about it and my sister at eight is too young; she has already seen more than she should.

It's about a year or so later; my mother is in the kitchen. She has found out that my father has yet again secretly sent money to his sister and mother in Sri Lanka. She shouts at him for hours, and my sister and I are in our rooms trying to pretend that nothing is happening. We hear her cry out and when we rush in, we see streaks of pink all over the floor. He has taken the rusted tin of sugar and brought it down hard on her head. Her skin has split, blood welling and gushing. Together they go to the hospital where they will say that she hit her head on a cabinet. I send my weeping sister to her room. I clean up the blood, the glistening sugar, the pink swirls where they have mixed. I think, this is my mother's blood, and feel woozy. By the time they come home the kitchen is clean.

When it was particularly bad, I would take my sister and we would leave. It didn't matter how late it was; we would wander through those empty suburban streets. Often we would leave so quickly we were barefoot, the concrete cooling under our feet. In the park we would swing up toward the moon, drunk with the freedom of being outside while the other kids were all in bed. We would steal into gardens and pluck roses, hydrangeas, lilies. Hours later I would slip up to our door and put my ear to it. If there was still screaming, we would keep walking. We would only come back when they were asleep. We would fill all the vases in the house with stolen flowers. The scent would permeate the house and perfume our dreams. In the morning my father would lecture us for stealing other people's property. He was always so concerned about other people, how we looked to them, what we stole from them. He never seemed to care about what was taken from us.

A Bad Arranged Marriage

Outside the house we were perfect. Inside the house we were sometimes tranquil, sometimes happy. Other times, perhaps much less often, we were terrified. The problem was that we never knew which mother we would have, which parents we would have: the predictable parents who made us study and who we knew loved us, or the ones who violently raged at each other and caught us up in their maelstrom. We were experts in reading their moods, always on guard for the moment when the darkness returned.

I knew from very early on that the problem was a bad arranged marriage. My mother told me that she had been married off too young to a terrible man ten years older than her. She told me all about how badly my father treated her, how he didn't love her, how much she hated him. It was confusing sometimes because I knew that I looked like him, that I had inherited many of his qualities, and that he was often sweet to me. She hated him and I was half him, so I also knew that some part of myself was disgusting, worthy of hatred. I also knew it was my job to make peace between my parents and keep them safe from each other.

Divorce was unthinkable. Our unspoken agreement was that my parents should never have been married but now that they had and now that we, the children, had arrived, there was no escape for any of us.

When we arrived in America, I realized that divorce was normalized; there were even Sri Lankans we knew who had gotten divorced and had started new lives. There was some stigma but it wasn't impossible the way it had been in South Asia and in Africa. At thirteen I told my parents they should get divorced. I was astounded when they did not. It took me decades to understand that the narrative of a bad arranged marriage was only a veil for something far harder to see.

Scar

Over the years, often due to me begging, or threatening to cut off contact, my mother has gone to therapy. But always, in about the fourth month, when the hard work of introspection starts, she leaves.

There's also a cultural reason for her distrust. Traditionally South Asian families consider mental health problems shameful, possibly contagious. When my mother was a teenager, the prettiest cousin of her generation started having what sounds like psychotic fits. Her parents took her abroad for treatment but when none of it seemed to work, they returned to Sri Lanka and locked her away in the family house. People knew she was in the house—they could even hear her shouting upstairs—but no one was allowed to see her. This internment lasted for three decades. In certain South Asian communities the madwoman in the attic is not just a Gothic horror story but is a distinct possibility for a woman undergoing psychological problems. In the aftermath of her own rages, when she had alienated loved ones or broken property, my mother used to call me crying. She'd say over and over, "I'm not crazy." It translates to "Don't lock me up. Don't throw away the key."

Instead of therapy my mother puts her faith in ritual. As children we were repeatedly taken to the temple where a Hindu priest held up a hundred limes one by one to our foreheads and sliced through them with a cutter. The juice was supposed to squirt into the evil eye of those unknown enemies who were causing us unhappiness. To this day my mother will email and ask if she can send us good-luck charms blessed by holy men. She says she has had our horoscopes read and that I must wear pink, my sister must wear gold to keep us safe from malignant influences. She is perpetually hopeful that if we just adhered to these constantly changing rules, we would be a happy family.

When I was seventeen, my parents took us to rural India to the enormous ashram of their guru, Sai Baba, a holy man who has millions of devotees around the world. We lived in a family shed, a huge crowded structure. We slept on mats on the floor and ate in a giant cafeteria. We woke at 3:30 a.m. and my mother, my sister, and I sat on the ground, on the female side, hundreds of thousands of women all around us in the predawn dark, waiting for the guru to emerge. When he came out, the women burst into song. As he swept past us my mother handed him a letter detailing all her woes. She wept with devotion as he took it from her.

I didn't give a shit about the guru. I hated the place, the rules, the food. I hated the segregation of men and women. I had a boyfriend in America but other cute boys lived in our shed, including two brothers from South Africa. While my parents napped in the midday heat, I went to their corner and we sat on the ground cutting mangoes. When one of them flipped the knife into the air, I instinctively reached out to catch it and the blade sank deep into the meat of the two middle fingers on my right hand almost to the bone. The blood came quick and fast.

All I could think about was how angry my mother would be. I begged the boys and their parents not to tell her. I clutched a toilet-paper roll and then another and turned them soggy. I bled down the front of my yellow shalwar chemise. People gathered all around me; old women were whispering that I had been punished for speaking to boys. Someone told my mother and when she came, her face was cold and angry. She didn't say anything to me. She turned and walked away. Someone wrapped up my hand, and my father walked with me to the hospital. At the door of that crowded, chaotic place we realized he couldn't come inside with me because the building was gender segregated, so I walked the halls of that hospital where I didn't speak the language alone. Eventually I found a doctor to sew me up. She was a surgeon and she only had huge, black internal-medicine thread so that after she was finished, my two fingers looked like a row of enormous spiders were holding my skin together.

When I returned from the hospital, my mother ignored me. I had defied the queen and therefore I didn't exist. Her angry silence went on for days. Twenty-eight years later, I still have the scar of that cut. It reminds me of how it feels to need comfort and instead find rage. It reminds me that in moments of pain I will never turn to her for comfort because she, hurt child as she is, will never be able to give it to me.

Surviving

This is how I survived my childhood: I disappeared. As a child I slipped into books, and everything around me, including my own body, faded away. It was a very conscious act. I am very lucky that early and unknowingly, I found books instead of any other drug. I've never fully returned from that early dissociation. My deepest life has been spent inside books, both in the consumption and later in the creation of them, and in this way perhaps my mother's condition has been the primary shaping force in my life.

As an adolescent I saw that our Sri Lankan–Angeleno community looked like the perfect model minority, but behind the manicured lawns, the luxury cars, and multiple degrees were various levels of rot. Daughters I knew whispered that their fathers had touched them and everyone shushed them up. Girls I knew were married off to men twenty-five years their senior by their mothers and no one intervened. As long as you achieved the American dream, nothing that happened inside these houses mattered.

In this atmosphere I learned to lie. It astounds me how quickly this happened. At twelve she was wiping my butt and five years later I was sneaking out of the house to have sex with my first boyfriend. By American standards my behavior was normal. By Sri Lankan standards I was out of control. Mothers told their daughters not to talk to me. An uncle called my parents and said I had been seen with a boy. My parents tried to reassert control but it was too late and soon after I left home for college.

In the years after, I consistently chose partners who were less emotionally healthy than me. I knew the savior role intimately. Even though I had left home and moved to the Bay Area, I would visit my parents' house often. When my mother went to Sri Lanka for vacations, I would go to LA and run her business for months. I lived in her house, wore her clothes, essentially *became* her. When I was back in the Bay, I would talk to her on the phone almost daily. She told me her troubles; often she sobbed. I would modulate my voice into a peaceful tone that I didn't use with anyone else. I would talk quietly and gently. Often my entire body hurt before I called her but I ignored this. If I didn't talk her down, terrible things could happen. I was sure that if I just found the right tool for her—meditation, a book, a counselor that she liked—she would be happy. I would save her. It was all up to me. I had escaped the prison walls of my childhood but I carried that prison inside me well into adulthood.

Saving My Own Life

I met the man who would eventually become my husband in 2007. Whit was the first person to tell me that my childhood sounded dysfunctional, that I almost always cried after talking to my mother, that I returned from trips home emotionally wrecked and in physical pain, and that every single time he and I planned a trip, I had to cancel or almost cancel because my parents had gotten into a violent fight or one of them had threatened suicide. I had barely registered these events as unusual. Yes, my family was chaotic, but what could I do? To his concerns, I said, "You don't understand. You're white. This is just how it works in South Asian families."

I loved this man but I didn't understand him. He wanted a love that was deep and peaceful. But if you didn't rage, wasn't that a sign that you didn't love each other? I spent the first part of our relationship waiting for him to shout at me. It took about four years before I realized he just never was going to do that. I was astounded by this realization. It took many more years to relax into this safety.

In those early years of our relationship, I was a feral child in the arena of love. I wept, I screamed, I was insanely jealous. If he spent time with friends, let alone a girl, my entire body flew into panic and pain; I felt like I was going to die. One day we spent the morning together and he said he was going to watch football with his friends and would see me for dinner. After he left I sat in my car and scream-cried for three hours. I was hysterical, but by the time he was available again I was perfectly fine. I scared myself that day. I knew something was very wrong. I knew that if I didn't do something, we would break up, but much worse than that, I would carry these behaviors into every future relationship. I would spend my life ruled by uncontrollable sorrow and rage. I would waste my one wild and precious life.

Rewiring My Brain

What ensued in the next five years was a journey toward healing that continues into the present. It involved ripping up the neural networks that had been laid down in my brain in childhood and remained there for over thirty years and replacing them, one by one, with something new. As with any ripping, it was excruciating.

Years-long engagement with three tools helped me save my own life: Vipassana meditation, which allowed me access into my own body; Co-Dependents Anonymous, which showed me that the behaviors that let me survive childhood were not serving me anymore; and the guidance of a skilled therapist who reparented me into adulthood.

The other thing that saved me was being in a long-term romantic relationship. I tantrummed for years and when I was done, Whit was still there. With him I had all the emotions I had not been allowed to have as a child, because for the first time, I knew I was safe. Some deep part of me recognized that I could trust him, even though I didn't consciously believe this until years later. He came into our relationship with understanding and compassion already in his bloodline, and I could not have asked for a better partner in the lifework of love.

Another Explanation

My therapist and I had worked together for years before he said, "Your mother could be a borderline," and a door swung open. What if her "moods" were not just marital problems but a diagnosable personality disorder, something that could be qualified and discussed? I know I can't diagnose my mother. I know it's extremely complicated to reach a diagnosis even when one works closely with a therapist. But what I can say is that when I read about this condition, for the first time in my life, the disparate pieces of my childhood fell into place. For the first time I felt both hope for myself and compassion for my mother.

The website borderlinepersonalitytreatment.com lists the following as baseline symptoms of borderline personality disorder (a condition contracted in childhood by abandonment, abuse, or death): neglect, overcontrol, rage, criticism, blame, enmeshment, parental alienation.

Borderline Personality Disorder

Learning about BPD was a revelation. The most insightful book for me was *Understanding the Borderline Mother: Helping Her Children Transcend the Intense, Unpredictable, and Volatile Relationship* by Christine Ann Lawson. On every page I found my family. The book described my mother's often uncanny behavior with an almost impossible precision. It explained how we worked together as a family to manage, excuse, and ignore what was happening inside our house. It explained how my father enabled. It explained how my sister and I were respectively cast as the all-good and all-bad child, both labels coming with dangerous repercussions.

The book gave me a greater insight into my own life than any book I had ever read. For the first time I felt like what I had experienced in childhood was not a fragment of my imagination. This paragraph is underlined in both my copies of the book: "Children of borderlines have been down the rabbit hole. They have heard the Queen of Hearts order everyone beheaded. They have attended the mad tea party and argued with the Duchess for the right to think their own thoughts. They grow weary of feeling big one minute and small the next."[1]

Most important, I learned that as the "all bad" firstborn daughter of a borderline mother, I had been at risk for developing the

---

[1]Christine Ann Larson, *Understanding the Borderline Mother: Helping Her Children Transcend the Intense, Unpredictable, and Volatile Relationship*, New York, Rowan & Littlefield, 2004, p. 278.

illness myself. It was only through the modeling of other adults and an immersion in literature that I had escaped with less dire and reversible symptoms.

As I read, I agonized about whether to tell my mother. It felt like knowing that someone was a diabetic and then keeping that information to myself. It felt unfair not to tell her but terrifying to tell her. Then one day on the phone with her, the words came out of my mouth spontaneously. I said I had learned about this condition and that it was not her fault but I thought she might have it. She didn't get angry; she was receptive. I asked her if I could read her the list of symptoms and she said yes. I read her a list of thirty symptoms. Repeatedly she said, "No, I don't have that one." Then I would remind her of a scenario in which she had exhibited that behavior until we had checked off almost every single box.

I asked if I could send her information and she said yes, and so I sent her a box of books about the condition. She said she received them, and I would try to talk to her about them, ask her if she had read them, and she would brush the questions away. I stopped asking and she never again mentioned the books, not once in the decade that followed. When I do visit my parents—these days, a very rare occasion—I see these books on the living room bookshelf side by side with our childhood books, our college textbooks, just another layer of detritus gathering in the house. She must be loath to throw them out since I gave them to her. Yet she has never been able to grapple with the fact that so many of the behaviors that seem inexplicable to her may have a name.

I think that I understand my mother so much better now. I know that even as she hurts people she is hurting exponentially more. I've watched videos of borderlines in recovery on YouTube explain what it feels like to have a brain that relentlessly attacks the self. Borderlines often have unbearable self-loathing and despair. I recognize that when my mother locked herself away in the shower for hours when we were growing up, she was desperately trying to manage her violent psychic pain.

I've watched a borderline in recovery say, "I would be so cruel. I would make people I loved hurt. I would spew venom at them and see how they were hurt by my words and it would hurt me but I couldn't stop. It was as if I wanted to keep hurting myself through them."[2] My mother, too, couldn't seem to stop. She, too, seemed to hurt herself by hurting those she loves. She was terrified of driving people away but she could not stop herself from doing the very thing that made people leave. The only way to protect oneself from this onslaught was to leave her presence. As *Understanding the Borderline Mother* put it, "The greatest protection the adult child of a borderline has is the ability to leave."[3]

Borderline personality disorder is not curable. No drugs have been found to be effective. However, long-term therapy with a skilled and dedicated professional focused on learning to manage

---

[2]Recovery Mum, "I Felt Like a Child All the Time," YouTube video, 10:52, December 2016, https://youtube.com/watch?v=eoqy3WM7YO0.

[3]Christine Ann Larson, *Understanding the Borderline Mother: Helping Her Children Transcend the Intense, Unpredictable, and Volatile Relationship*, New York, Rowan & Littlefield, 2004, p. 278.

symptoms can lead to a much better quality of life, especially in the realm of interpersonal relationships. My mother has never sought long-term ongoing therapy.

Memory

Once when I visited my parents' home I found a long list taped to the microwave. My dad had listed all the times my mother had humiliated him in public, self-harmed, verbally abused his family, shouted at someone else in the last month. The incidents were dated. He was intuitively attempting to manage her illness and make her remember those moments when she had hurt him deeply in the hope that she would treat him better.

Incidents that are seared in my mind as well as my sister's and my father's were often completely lost to my mother's memory. I didn't understand this discrepancy until I read the following: "Studies show that chronically intense emotions damage the part of the brain responsible for memory. . . . Because the borderline mother is unable to remember intensely emotional events, *she is unable to learn from experience* [my italics]. She may repeat destructive behaviors without remembering previous consequences."[4]

This is the saddest part of our story. My mother remembers a different life than the one we've lived with her. The chasm

[4]Christine Ann Larson, *Understanding the Borderline Mother: Helping Her Children Transcend the Intense, Unpredictable, and Volatile Relationship*, New York, Rowan & Littlefield, 2004, p. 278.

between us is unbridgeable because she often, though not always, cannot remember why a loved one might be hurt and therefore need to emotionally and physically withdraw from her.

My own memory is also spotty and broken. The day before her wedding, my sister, Namal, and I sat in her best friend's kitchen talking about our childhoods. I said, "Remember this?" And my sister would say, "Oh yeah, I forgot about that." Then she would say, "Remember when this happened?" And a memory would leap like a flame into the front of my mind. Her friend sat silent and finally said, "You guys are talking like it wasn't a big deal. This is absolutely insane stuff." We looked at her, startled; we hadn't thought of it as particularly dysfunctional. So much had happened that we normalized what others would not and forgot what most other people would not forget. In this essay I've only talked about a few of the memories that are crystal clear. There is a fog of others. It has been one of the greatest blessings of my life that my sister is able to mirror my experience.

Breaking Away

Eventually I realized that to reclaim my life I would need to emotionally separate from my parents. Six years ago I told them that I would be engaging with them less, and if they talked about the other partner, I would ask them to stop and if they continued, I would hang up.

There were months of struggle as I tried to break away. My father called and said my mother was so upset I wasn't talking to her that she had locked herself in the bathroom and he was afraid she was self-harming. He passed her the phone through the crack and I listened as she sobbed and babbled in a child's voice. At some point she said "I love you" over and over, hundreds of times, in the little girl's voice. I don't know if she was saying it to me or to herself or to someone else. I spoke in the old soothing voice until she was coherent and then when I finally hung up, I was exhausted, my entire body hurt, and I was furious with myself for not being able to assert my boundary.

Months later my father called and said in a broken voice, "I can't take it anymore. I'm going to do something bad." I begged him to hold on as I was in the mountains with bad phone reception. I hung up and then I drove like a banshee down the mountain, calling over and over and getting no answer. Images of his body bleeding on the kitchen floor or prone in their shared bed flashed through my mind. I called my cousin Dinesh, who lives in Sri Lanka and has been my lifelong confidant. "Call the police," he said. I called Whit. "Call the police," he said. So despite my own fears about how law enforcement deals with bodies of color, I called the police and talked to an officer who said, "Oh yes. I know that house. I've been there before." I hung up and called my dad again. He answered and said he had gone on a walk to clear his head after a big fight. He was fine now. He asked me why I sounded upset; then he said, "Wait, there's someone at the door," and then, "It's the police." I said, "Yes, I called them because I didn't know if you had killed yourself." He said, "Why did you do that? The neighbors will see."

They kept him in a facility for three days. When he came out, he said he had talked to a therapist and it was the best thing that had happened to him because someone had actually listened to him. I asked him if he'd continue. He said no because everyone knows therapists are crooks. If their patients get better, they stop getting paid.

That was my breaking point. If they weren't willing to save their own lives, I wasn't going to drown with them.

Love

I don't know if the behaviors I saw as a child continue in the house I grew up in. I hope that as they age my parents have found some peaceful coexistence. I do think that they have been able to reinvent themselves as really good grandparents to my sister's children. As I said before, I see them very infrequently these days. Any more than a few hours in their company and I am assailed by the insurmountable mountain of what we cannot talk about. In their company I find myself turning mute, surly, rude. I become a different person than I know myself to be, a different person than my close ones know me to be. The burden of the unsaid turns my heart into a balled fist.

It's important that I also say this: in many ways my mother and father were very good parents. In the various moments that I refused to fulfill the scripted role of a traditional South Asian daughter, they were supportive in ways that most South Asian parents are not. They were always financially generous. Unlike most of my friends, I never had to work in college; I was able to graduate debt-free, a tremendous gift in these days when student debts cripple lives. They took us traveling to places my peers had never even imagined. In an incredible act of largesse, my father recently helped Whit and me buy a house. When I was struggling to sell my first book, my mother sent me checks whenever she could and let me stay in her house in Sri Lanka when I was there. In all these ways, they are sweet and giving people. I know this and I hold it as part of our collective truth. I am sure that my breaking of the silence around my childhood will feel profoundly ungrateful to them. So I need to say I am very grateful for their many gifts.

When I make a rare visit to the house in which I grew up, I see dozens of pictures of my sister and me, almost all of them from childhood or adolescence. As if clocks stopped then. I know my parents love and miss me. I, too, deeply mourn all that we lost. But I have reached the bottom of my own particular well. There is compassion here but not much hope for connection beyond that.

When I leave my childhood house, my parents stand outside, waving. She on the front steps, he on the edge of the lawn. They wave and wave as I drive away. They will not go into the house until they lose sight of me. They keep waving until they are very small, like tiny children, in my rearview mirror and then they are gone.

Then slowly I can remember that I have made a different path for myself. I have found the ones who know my heart and keep it safe. I have created myself as someone who, on most days,

I like, respect, and love. I have made my way into myself and learned that *love, too, is contagious.* I have learned that healing is possible. That we can make lives that we couldn't even have imagined when we were little and that we can carry the little ones who we were into these new and luminous lives.

Postscript: Six months before this essay was due to be published, I sent it to my mother. This is the email she sent back: "Duwa, I am so proud of you for having the strength to publish this essay! It is going to help a lot of other people. I am very sorry for what took place in our life. I take full responsibility. I cannot change the past!!! I love you very much and hope we can move forward to build a better relationship in the future. I am proud of all your awesome achievements. Love you, Ammi."

All About My Mother

By Brandon Taylor

My mother didn't share much of herself with anyone. There's this idea that Southern families are full of stories, but mine wasn't. Or, I guess, my family was full of stories, but they didn't share them, or if they did, the stories came with so high a price that we often didn't speak for days after divulging them.

Once, my mother told me that when I was very little, I wouldn't give up my pacifier. She had tried to break me of it when I was one and then again when I was two, but I wouldn't. She said that I carried it with me everywhere and sucked and sucked on it, wouldn't let it out even to sleep. She said that she tried taking it from me when I took my bottle, but that I held it clutched tight in my hand. She could have pried it from my fingers easily.

I was a baby, after all, and so could not have resisted her, but her strength failed her again and again at the crucial moment. She pulled on it, and I held it tight in my mouth or my hand, and my eyes filled with fat tears, and I began to make a hiccuping sound, like swallowing something too big for my body. She pulled, and I resisted, and she didn't have it in her to take it from me.

But one day my stomach was upset. I had always had an uneasy stomach. Something about me was always hot and feverish, something always upsetting my belly. But on this day, I went into the bathroom alone and threw up, and she came in after me because I was pitched forward into the bowl. She looked down and saw that I was trying to pull my pacifier back out of the vomit. She saw her chance and flushed it away.

She told me that story for the first time on my birthday when I was turning five, I think. Everyone was in the room laughing at me—at the boy I was, or at the toddler I had been, I couldn't tell—and she was standing at the counter in the old trailer we lived in together. She put her hand on her hip and shook her head. Then she said, "You were always like that. Greedy." I felt stung by that comment. I had started putting on weight. I was in husky clothes already. She said it again for good measure, repeated it: "Greedy, greedy." Her voice rode the swell of the laughter in the room, and I sat on the floor playing with the toy a cousin's father had bought for me. My face grew hot. And she shook her head again. "You're spoiled," she said. Spoiled. Greedy. Someone called me Fat Albert, and the name stuck because my father's name was Alvin, and they sometimes called him Albert.

And I was husky. Fat Albert. That was the gift she gave me on my birthday. That and hot dogs that had been boiled too long and split down the middle on slices of white bread.

I find the story remarkable for many reasons, chief among which is the fact that my mother couldn't bring herself to take my pacifier. It amazes me, this act of grace and charity. I wondered at the time what had happened to turn her from someone who wouldn't take a pacifier from a crying baby into someone who called me greedy on my birthday for eating candy and cake. She often repeated the story, and the second thing that I find remarkable about it is how consistent the story was. When my mother told other stories, they always changed, inflected by her mood or by whatever point she was trying to support with it.

When I was very young, my mother worked as a housekeeper for a local motel. Neither of my parents drove—my mother because she had driven off the road once years before and had developed a complex about it and my father because he was legally blind—and so we didn't own a car. To get to work, my mother caught a ride with one of my aunts or paid her brother-in-law five dollars to take her and five dollars to pick her up. At the time, we were living on an acre and a half of formerly swampy dirt and cleared brush that sat at the back of my grandparents' land. My parents never owned any land of their own, and the trailer had been inherited from my grandmother's sister, who had moved across the property line to live at the bottom of a red-clay hill on my great-grandmother's land. It's odd to think about it now, how all of my relatives had clustered together that way, how the children never bought land of their own and stayed with their parents until they were too old or their families were too large and they dropped like overripe fruit into the yard. But it was convenient for my parents, who, as I said, didn't drive.

My mother worked because my father couldn't. I've never asked him what it is that he can see, though I've tested the limits of his sight indirectly, the way children often test the range of their parents' love. I would wait until he was standing still or sitting in a room alone. It was important that he was alone because I didn't want someone else to call out my name or give the game away. I'd stand just off to the side, or just far enough in the hall, waiting for him to turn toward me. I held myself perfectly still, thinking that if I didn't breathe or move or make the floor under me groan, he couldn't use his ears to find me. Sometimes, he'd come into my room and look, briefly, and even if he looked right at me, he didn't see me. He'd walk into my room, call my name, but not the way you call someone you're looking at, to draw them to attention. It was the voice you use when you're searching for someone, when you're facing a wall of trees that hold something you need out of your sight, and you have to call it, hoping it'll come to you, hoping it will rise from whatever place it's sleeping and sweep back toward you like the wind. He'd come into my room and say my name, and then, not seeing me, walk out again. And I'd be right there on the bed or on the floor, right in front of his face. My mother worked, and so we were alone a lot. Another game I liked to play was to wait until his voice grew hoarse and he was tired of saying my name, and then come up behind him and press my face against his damp lower back, and squeeze his sides and say, "I'm right here; you missed me."

And he'd groan and grumble and reach down and pinch me and say, "I missed you, all right."

When my mother came home in the late afternoon, she had no patience. She would call my name one time, and I felt something hard and cold shoot down my spine. I'd run into whatever room she was in, and she'd already be looking at me like she was mad about something. Her eyes were exceptionally dark and narrow. Her hair was black, and before she shaved her head in my teenage years, it was permed and in a bob of some kind. She wore no jewelry for most of her life. She had a kind of brutal mystery about her, as if nothing stuck to her, could stand to be near her without being torn or blasted into fragments.

I remember how the air turned dark and cold whenever she was around, and how I was afraid she'd hit me for something I had failed to account for, something that she scented in the air. My mother was not the kind of person who played games with children. Even when she tried to laugh with us, I always felt the edge of her ridicule stabbing my sides. When I first heard her weight on the steps outside, I'd hop up from bed and press my face to the window, and I'd watch as she mounted the stairs one at a time, their dusty solidity shaking under her as she lumbered into our home.

• • •

She sometimes had plastic bags with her, filled with misplaced and discarded things from other people's lives. She brought pillows from the hotel where she worked. She brought an array of chargers and cords. She brought, occasionally, toys or shirts. At another time in my life, she worked at a hotel attached to a golf course in my hometown. And she'd bring all sorts of things home, more expensive things: MP3 players, cameras, brand-name golf polo shirts, soaps and shampoos, things that looked out of place in the trailer where we lived. It was as if she were trying to lift us out of that place one item at a time, as if one can become better that way, rather than be made more acutely aware of one's place by the curious gravity exerted by objects drawn into our orbit.

I have a brother, though my earliest memories do not contain him. He's always been outdoors, roaming around, thumping under the house or vanishing off into the woods. Because of the way things turned out, I'm amazed at the remarkable tenderness contained in these early memories, their gray hues, but, I guess, what I find most remarkable is something that other people might find ordinary: my parents kept me at home during the first years of my life. That's why they have this fenced-in quality to them in memory. I wasn't allowed to go beyond the yard.

When I got to be five or six, this limitation extended to the road. That is, I was allowed to leave my yard and to wander into my grandparents' yard. I was allowed to plunge through the briars and the trees, leap over the clay banks of the ravine, or else slide down its slippery edges into the kudzu valley that grew all over the bits of cars in the ditch. But I was not allowed to cross the road to visit my father's sister, who was known to me as someone who gave me toys and gifts and played with me and let me comb her hair. I could only visit her when my dad took my hand and helped me cross. Something else that sticks out from this time is how I never tried to lose his hand and run ahead of him. I never jerked my hand down and squirmed or fought him in the road. I never tried to harm my father at all. When I look at children in the streets, I see them testing their independence, trying to run away from their parents. I see them slipping from their fingers, darting here or there, into the street, the world so empty of danger until the very moment a car comes sliding out of nowhere and suddenly the world is much smaller and much vaster all at the same time.

But not me. I held on to my dad's hand when we crossed the road. Or, I would ask my grandmother to take me across in search of my dad. The one time I crossed the road without permission, my mother had gone to town to buy me shoes for big-boy school. I would be starting first grade in a few weeks. And I'd felt emboldened by this. And I'd run across the road to see my aunt. I stood there at the bottom of her hill, and I huffed up it, and I waved to her when she got out of her car after work. And she fed me a snack. She fed me grapes. And let me watch cartoons; then she walked me back home. And my mother was waiting for me. Or, rather, they told me that she had bought me something and it was waiting in one of the back bedrooms at my grandmother's house. And I picked up the box of shoes on the bed, and out from behind the curtain that hung in front of the closet came my mother, suddenly, there, fierce and giant, and she took me hard by the arm and hit me over and over and over. And then she took the shoes away and said I'd have to go to school barefoot if I thought I was so grown.

But it's remarkable to me that before that, when I was tiny, a baby, really, a toddler, they kept me at home. It seems like the sort of gesture that is unfathomably tender. The sort of thing that you do when you love someone. And that's the thing I have a hard time with. They loved me enough to keep me at home when I was four. They loved me enough not to let me go down the stairs by myself. They held my hand and down we went.

The first thing that my father said to me when my mother died was that she had loved me. And at the time, I thought, what a ridiculous thing to say. Not because her love was evident to me—it was not and is not, really, an evident thing—but because he thought it meant so much to me and I felt at the time that it didn't. I scoffed and made a joke and he said it again: *She loved you. You know that, right? She loved you.*

It wasn't the sort of thing that we said in my family. My family was a series of hushed rages behind shut doors. We didn't say *I love you* or *good night* or *good morning.* The very act of speaking felt strained and hard. To say anything at all felt like putting the most vulnerable part of yourself on the table. But I talked anyway. Not out of bravery or anything like that, but out of stupidity, which is how children talk, anyway. We make noise that has no meaning. But my father took to saying it after my mother died, and I made a big show of not returning the words. I thought, we've played the game this long according to one set of rules, and I don't see a point in changing them.

But lately, I've begun to wonder if this isn't just my feeling as the baby of the family, the brat, the pain in the neck. All those years, I thought I was playing a trick on my dad, by pretending I wasn't there, by holding myself back, thinking myself invisible.

How like the selfish child to think that he's the one in charge, and to miss entirely that a father might pretend not to see you if he knew it would bring you joy to sneak up on him.

You miss a lot in first sight.

My mother died in 2014, four years before I sat down to write this piece. She had cancer for a short, intense time. I struggled with how to describe that. I did not want to say *battle* because it was not a battle exactly. She had cancer. And then she died from it. But we don't have a word for that, the time we spend with an illness knowing it will likely kill us. She had lung cancer, grown from an esophageal tumor, or so that's the story. I never know what to make of stories in my family, how many of them are true or made-up to resolve a discordant note. But I do know she had cancer and that she is now dead, has been dead for a few years.

Before my mother died, I didn't write very much nonfiction. Even the essays I turned in for school were halfhearted. It's the way you get to be when you're raised in a family with a testy relationship to facts. I don't mean *truth* exactly because I do think they told the truth in the best way they knew how. I mean *facts*, the things that we assume comprise the truth. One example: When I was very little, I asked my grandfather if there were baby chicks in the eggs collected from the chicken yard. He told me no, that the eggs we eat come from roosters, who are boys, and therefore cannot lay eggs with chicks in them. I believed that for a long time. And when I found out it was not true, I asked him about it. And he shrugged. He said, "Well, isn't that something."

Here is another example: When my mother was diagnosed with cancer, she told me the doctor gave her the choice between chemo and hospice and she lingered on the word *hospice* and laughed. She said, *I'm a fighter. I fight.* When my grandmother told me the story later, she said that it had been hard to convince my mother not to go into hospice, that she had all but signed the paperwork to wait out her death. Another story: The last conversation I had with my mother was about how annoying my brother was, how he called her and called her, wouldn't let her rest because he wanted to bother her, get under her skin, irritate her. My brother told me he'd been on the phone with her when she'd told him that she loved him and she began to cry and cry. They didn't talk about me at all.

I find it difficult to wrangle facts. I find it difficult to know what to do with them, how to organize them so they make sense and tell some sort of narrative. Truth is the thing that emerges from the careful arrangement of details. Fact is the word we use to describe a detail that has some particular relationship to the truth.

But any group of details can be arranged so they seem to cohere into a truth—and when we have discerned that truth, we call those details facts, even if they previously were untrue. I had a difficult time with essays because facts always felt so slippery to me. My family believed in ghosts and hauntings—that if you slept on your back, a witch would climb on top of you and strangle you or curse you, that if you went to bed after eating too much pork or salt, the devil would enter your room, slit your dreams, and enter them. What was I to do with essays and their order, their tidiness, their directness, when the only things I knew had to do with obscurity and the indirect? Take love, for another example, which to some people is expressed via touch or via words or some other means of affection. In my family, love was the slow accumulation of moments in which I was not subjected to great harm.

What is love if you get it secondhand? Is it a fact or merely a detail?

I am more comfortable in fiction than in nonfiction. In fiction, you get to decide what is real and not real, what is true and not true, which details are facts and which are mere detail. In fiction, I am the discerning eye, the single source of truth. But when I tried to write about my mother, all my stories were flat. I couldn't move her into fictional language, it seemed. Indeed, my journals about the days she died are full of details about the weather and the feeling that a chasm had opened up in me. I was trying in those early days to pin something down, to assemble a body of details that might give me some hint or clue of how to go on. I also felt that I had no right to feel that way, so sad about her, after all the hateful things I'd thought about her or been subjected to by her hands.

Here are some details about my mother: She once made me wipe under my arms in front of company because she said I was musty and smelled; she once opened a journal I was keeping under the bed and read it out in front of a party; she called me titty baby and sissy baby and made fun of the way I talked; she once attempted to empty out my bank account using blank checks she'd found in my closet; she told me that she needed two hundred dollars to buy school supplies for my niece but used the money to buy Natural Light instead; one time, she got into such a frenzy whipping me that she broke the light overhead and then made me pick the glass from my bedsheets in the dark. She was universally beloved by her friends. She had the sort of personality that people are drawn to—she could listen for hours, she had an encyclopedic knowledge of neighborhood gossip, and she was funny, could skewer you with an observation so keen and true that even if it was about you, you had to laugh. She was generous with her time. She wanted a lot of the world, and it had so little to offer her. She wanted to die, but my grandmother wouldn't let her.

The thing that kept me from writing about her, about grief, in fiction was that I lacked genuine, human feeling for my mother. Or, no, that's not true exactly. What I lacked was empathy for her. I was so interested in my own feelings about her that I couldn't leave room for her feelings or for what she wanted out of life.

I couldn't leave a space for her to be a person. I think, ultimately, other people aren't real to us until they're suffering or gone. That's when the imagination begins to work, trying to sort things out, trying to get them right, to understand them. I couldn't write fiction because I hadn't yet mastered my own feelings. I couldn't write fiction because I had not yet come to understand her or what her life had meant to her. I was solipsistic and righteous in my anger, my fear, my sadness. I missed all of the eerie symmetries between us—her trauma, my trauma, her rape, my rape, her anger, my anger. It's not that I came to love her really. But I did learn to extend to her the same grace that my friends extended to me. That's one of the beautiful things about writing, the way we learn about others and what that tells us about ourselves.

I think one of the hardest things to do in writing is to set aside the selecting intelligence that governs a piece and let another take over. When you write about the suffering of others, particularly the suffering of people to whom you are close, you must subjugate yourself, let yourself be subsumed into them. You can't be waiting for them to finish so that you can quickly say how much you agree and then add your own turn or twist. It's strange, really, that to grasp that which has hurt you, you must trust it not to hurt you when you let it inhabit you.

Do you know about baptism? How they hold you and lower you into the water? It's like that. You have to trust they'll lift you out.

Her name is Mary Jean Speigner. She died young. She worked

jobs so hard that the heels of her feet were cracked and gray. She dipped Skoal and spat it into Natural Light cans. She watched every soap opera religiously. Her favorite fish was whiting. She didn't eat salt. She didn't eat sugar. She fried her chicken black. She checked her blood sugar in the morning and in the afternoon, her blood purple red as she pressed it flat on the test slips. She had a tremor in her left hand. She had a pert nose and hooded, dark eyes. Her favorite color was green. Her favorite show was *Beverly Hills, 90210*. She loved Hugh Grant. She loved to laugh. Her favorite music was blues. She had a terrible singing voice but loved to sing. A man raped her when she was young, and nobody said anything about it. Nobody did anything about it. She saw him every day. She drank every day. Sometimes, she didn't eat because her stomach hurt so bad that she wanted to cry. But she didn't cry. She never cried. Just once. When her sister called her an ugly liar when they were full-grown. She went home and cried on the bed for hours. She hated bugs. Her voice was raspy. She hated to be touched. She hated to be spoken to like she was stupid. She hated secrets. She never told the truth. She danced all the time. She slept late. She stayed up late. She had trouble sleeping. She was afraid to hear about the dreams of other people; it was like a screeching sound to her, to hear about what other people had dreamed. She could make a joke out of anything. She loved to tell stories. She believed in magic. Nobody stood up for her so she had to stand up for herself, and after a while, she got tired of standing.

I wish I had gotten to know her better.
I think we would have been great friends.
I wish I had tried harder. Sooner.
This isn't enough. It'll never be enough.
But I have to stop for now.

I Met Fear on the Hill

By Leslie Jamison

It's the summer of 1966, and Sheila and Peter are a young married couple living in Berkeley. They are very much in love, and also very high—tripping on acid for the first time in their lives, in Tilden Park, walking in a shallow stream full of primordial monsters, or at least salamanders. The leaves are emeralds. The whole world is an amoeba. They are Adam and Eve, and they've found their way back to the garden.

They are renting a room in a communal house from a lawyer turned drug dealer; a local character named Wild Bill painted their walls during an acid trip: "Oh Lord, I could be bounded in a nutshell and count myself a king of infinite space, were it not that I have BAD DREAMS." They eat spaghetti made with pot pesto and cookies baked with pot butter. Drugs make their minds feel wrapped in rabbit fur. They go to dinner parties that turn into orgies. They have a wife-swap with a distinguished poet and his wife. They believe in liberating love from possession, but their open marriage starts buckling when Sheila falls in love with someone else.

This is the plot, more or less, of *The Parting of the Ways*, an unpublished novel written by a man named Peter Bergel in 1968. It's the story of two people who are young and passionate and broke and vulnerable, and it's the story—ultimately—of their shared future dissolving. It's also the story of my mother.

My mother before she was a mother has always lived in my mind as a collection of myths—half-invented, barely possible. Reading a novel in which she is a character simply literalized what already felt true: the years of her youth seemed larger than life.

My mom's name isn't Sheila. She hates the name Sheila. Her name is Joanne. She fell in love with Peter, who is actually named Peter, when she was a sophomore at Reed College. They got married after he graduated, a year before she did, and divorced two years after that. Their time together fascinated me—especially when they lived as hippies in Berkeley, trying to make their open marriage work—because I only knew my mother in the context of the ordinary days of my childhood, with NPR on the freeway commute and casseroles in the oven. My best friend said our fridge was always full of leftovers involving beans.

What can I tell you about my relationship with my mom? For

many years of my childhood, it was just the two of us. We made vegetarian sloppy joes for dinner. We watched *Murder, She Wrote* on Sunday nights, eating our two bowls of ice cream side by side. We did a ritual on New Year's Day that involved writing down our wishes and burning them with a candle flame. In many photos from my childhood, she is embracing me—one arm wrapped around my stomach, the other pointing at something, saying, Look at that, directing my gaze toward ordinary wonders. To talk about her love for me, or mine for her, would feel almost tautological; she has always defined my notion of what love is. Just like it's meaningless to say our ordinary days were everything to me, because they *were* me. They composed me. They still do. I don't know any self that exists apart from them.

How many times has my mom picked up the phone to hear my voice cracked with tears, only letting it crack once I knew she was there? When she arrived in the hospital after my daughter was born, I sat there on the starched sheets holding my baby, and she held me, and I cried uncontrollably—because I could finally understand how much she loved me, and I could hardly stand the grace of it.

When my mom told me that her first husband had written a novel about their marriage, I was thirty years old and feverish with curiosity. Peter and I didn't know each other well. He had been a benevolent figure hovering around the edges of my childhood, vaguely mythic himself, living in the Oregon woods. I knew he kept his income under the federal taxation minimum to avoid financing our nation's wars. I knew he'd been arrested for blocking access to nuclear power plants. I knew he'd given me a dream catcher when I was a kid.

Growing up, I had a cinematic portrait of their youthful marriage, painted in broad brushstrokes—full of acid, folk music, and heartbreak—and it thrilled me that some part of my mom's past lay beyond my grasp, far beyond the familiar landscape of our shared life of freeway exits and haggles over breakfast. But even as I felt a certain excitement at the fact that her youth lay beyond my vision, I also wanted to see it. This is part of why I turned it into myth—claimed it by making it into something reductive and vivid that I could hold in my hand like a jewel.

During my childhood and teenage years, I conjured a vague vision of my mom and Peter as a young couple from photographs and scraps of anecdotes: my mom was a leggy brunette with smoky hazel eyes and sculptural cheekbones, one of those infuriating women who are beautiful without particularly caring about being beautiful; while Peter was a tall guy with a beard and a dramatic, regal nose, the son of European Jewish intellectuals who had always identified as an outsider but had found his people in college, playing folk songs on his guitar and breaking the drama professor's rules by doing his set changes in character, as a lowly shoe shiner with a blacked-out tooth. My mom told me there was something primal about how she was drawn to him, as if she sensed he was the leader of the tribe.

When I wrote to Peter to ask if he would be willing to share his novel with me, he actually seemed excited to send it, even though there were only a few copies of the manuscript in existence. I waited eagerly for its arrival—wanting it to confirm my mythic ideas about my mother's past, but also hungry for it to grant that myth the breath and bones of particularity.

The novel arrived as loose pages tucked in a purple folder, the faded photocopy of an original typewriter manuscript. The pagination skipped backward partway through, a relic of the revision process, and the pages were peppered with small handwritten corrections. In a scene involving a few friends smoking pot and sticking their toes into liquid laundry detergent, an apostrophe was carefully crossed out.

The novel felt like precious contraband in my hands, as if I were reading letters I wasn't meant to see. I read it in a single day. It let me perch on my mother's shoulder as the mysterious, elusive, unknowable days of her early life played out in front of me, starting with that first trip in Tilden Park. I'd been a tiny stowaway tucked into her ovaries, a not-yet-person along for the ride.

The novel's opening chapters conjure paradise: Sheila and Peter ride a psychedelic painted pickup truck through the Emeryville mudflats, drinking orange juice laced with acid. They go to the Fillmore in San Francisco to watch Jefferson Airplane play with a band called the Grateful Dead, who haven't yet cut an album. California offers them a thrilling alternative to their existence back in Portland, where Peter worked at a stainless steel foundry, surrounded by coworkers picking their noses above the degreaser and quartering their powdered doughnuts in the break room. In California, their life revolves around what Peter calls the "Ethic of Cool," something ineffable but unmistakable: It's a wooden bowl of clean grass in the middle of the dining room table. It's people frequently and unironically calling things "far out." It's a beautiful girl named Darlene sweet-talking the cop who wants to write her up for trespassing on a state beach. Even if Peter doesn't fully understand what "cool" is, he knows it when he sees it. "Now I may not know much about sitar," he observes at one party, "but I can sure as HELL tell that this dude knows what he is doing."

Their Shangri-La is a nude beach down the coast, where they go camping one weekend. The only problem is the man with a shotgun guarding the private road. ("Paradise down there and we can't get to it. We're blocked by an insurmountable egomaniac who won't let us climb down his lousy cliff.") Luckily, a naked man standing in the surf draws them a map in the sand that leads them to a secret road. They make a campfire and spend the night, tripping at dusk near the glimmering phosphorescent algae. They hold a mock funeral for "the good old days." They don't realize they are living the good old days, the ones they will someday look back on, the ones a daughter might look back on, too—as if she is peering over the shoulders of their ghosts, hungry for the lives they once lived.

Trying to write about my mother is like staring at the sun. It feels like language could only tarnish this thing she has given me, my whole life—this love. For years, I've resisted writing about her. Great relationships make for bad stories. Expression naturally gravitates toward difficulty. Narrative demands friction, and my mom and I live—by the day, the week, the decade—in closeness. Besides, I'm no fool. Who wants to hear too much about someone else's functional parental relationships anyway?

A friend once told me that it was frankly a little bit exhausting to hear me talk about how much I loved my mother. But what can I say? My hunger for her feels endless. I want to love her more fully, by loving the woman she once was. Perhaps it's a way back into the womb, past the womb—seeking these stories of her, from before I was born.

Sheila and Peter's marriage starts to unravel halfway through *The Parting of the Ways*, after Sheila falls in love with an engineer named Earl. Earl is introduced as a hopeless straight man, reading the Stanford alumni newsletter on a stoop while everyone else in a ten-mile radius is getting impossibly high. But he and Sheila have a history—insofar as it's possible to have a history with someone when you are twenty-two years old. When the three of them go backpacking together in the Sierras, part of Peter's attempt *not* to be jealous, Peter finds himself haunted by images of Sheila and Earl together: "my subconscious opened a trapdoor to show me a weird little 3D film built out of my fears and insecurities." Even though Sheila and Peter have an open marriage, they aren't meant to fall in love with other people.

The rift caused by Sheila's relationship with Earl becomes a fissure opening onto deeper discontents: she and Peter can't quite make their life together work and can't quite agree on the life they want to lead. They are broke and trying to figure out what to do about it. Is Peter going to get a job? Is he going to get a job that requires cutting his long hair? The chapters stop being called things like "Consenting to Blow Your Mind" and "The Second Coming," and start being called things like "Hassles." They could have been kings of infinite space, but there's no running from their bad dreams.

Their tensions reach a boiling point at Sheila's mother's house in the suburbs. "Mother Jean" has asked Sheila and Peter if they'll take her on an acid trip. Grandma Pat? I thought as I was reading, then nodded with recognition at the exchange she has with Peter. When he warns her, "Acid isn't all hearts and flowers," she replies, "Neither am I." She is ready for anything—only disappointed when her first hallucination is of a boiled ham.

During that trip, Peter talks to Mother Jean about his fears that Sheila might want to end their marriage, and Sheila herself has a confrontation with fear behind her mother's house. "Fear and I had a little discussion up on top of the hill," Sheila tells Peter, just before asking him explicitly, finally, "Do you think we can stay together?"

As a reader, I followed the unraveling of their marriage with a sense of tender sadness mingled with selfish relief. Their marriage needed to fall apart, after all, in order for me to exist.

The novel's epigraph is from that famous poem by Robert Frost, who is identified as "a straight American poet":

Two roads diverged in a wood, and I—
I took the one less traveled by

I've always found the most moving part of that poem to be the stuttering pause created by the line break, the repetition of the pronoun—I / I—as if the speaker is trying to assure himself that his path was the right one. But there's a break in his own voice that betrays his uncertainty.

The fork in this road is starkly asymmetric: Sheila is determined to end the marriage, and Peter is devastated. His pain is operatic and eager to express itself. He writes a poem called "Rough Spot," full of barren imagery: "The strange ocular rain / Gets no one / Pregnant." He goes to Sexual Freedom League parties where you can have sex with strangers, but they aren't much fun. During their separation, he finds himself playing guitar at a party one night: "I reach into the open wound and bring the pain out like an eel wriggling on the end of a hook, hold it up, glory in it."

Sheila, on the other hand, is portrayed as unruffled: self-possessed and craving independence. When she tells Peter that she wants to get her own place, he sees the determination harden in a "firm little corner of her mouth." That firm-set mouth—her determination, her desire for autonomy—stands in contrast to his open wound. Reading *The Parting of the Ways*, however, I knew what its characters could not: that even after getting divorced, my mother and Peter would stay important to each other for more than fifty years. The end of their marriage was just the beginning of their story.

It was an act of trust for Peter to send me his novel. Not only am I his ex-wife's daughter—and thus, perhaps, a biased audience—but I'm also a writer, that particular species of vampire: one part barnacle, one part critic, always capable of betrayal. Someone invested in stories of my own.

But I don't think Peter would ever think of me as his "ex-wife's daughter," because he doesn't think of my mom as his "ex-wife." At one point, when Peter asked me what this essay was going to be about, I told him that I wanted to explore the ways that his marriage to my mom influenced the rest of both of their lives, as well as the ways their lives diverged after their relationship ended. He interrupted me midsentence to say, "The relationship never ended. I would never characterize it that way."

It came as a relief that I loved his novel as much as I did. I loved its details, how it evoked the world of that summer with crisp tenderness, in all its fever-dream wonder: friends letting their baby sleep in a dresser drawer as a bassinet, roommates keeping two pet mice who leave droppings all over the apartment, a guy writing a comic book about a hero whose superpower is that he can give anyone an acid trip (even the members of the jury who might convict him for drug possession!). I loved how the novel noticed the small things, how it recognized acid as a pretext and catalyst for lavish attention to the ordinary world, to the pleasurably aggressive sensation, for example, of drinking

Diet Rite soda: "The bubbles roll into my mouth like the tide coming, and each one has a little pitchfork that's driving into my tongue." I loved the novel's sense of awe—the startling way it describes listening to Coltrane "as if the music were concrete, it hardens in mid-pour into a bridge upon which I can walk straight up and out of my own head"—and its sense of absurdity, how one character suggests curing a bad case of crabs: "Shave half your pubes, pour kerosene on the other half, light it, and stab the little mothers as they run from the flames."

But the book is so much more than just a curiosity cabinet of hippie countercultural artifacts; it's ultimately an unapologetically earnest articulation of the hope and sense of possibility that bloom in the attempt to build a life with somebody, and the despair of watching that life crumble, watching that person pull away. I'd already seen my mother weather a divorce—from my father, when I was eleven—but reading about the end of her first marriage not only forced me to confront her as someone capable of causing pain, it also forced me to confront that her experience of divorcing my father, as much as we had discussed it, contained layers of hurt that lay beyond my sight—that I might never fully fathom.

In one sense, reading *The Parting of the Ways* felt like reading a stack of private letters—charged by the same transgressive thrill as snooping through your parents' drawers when you're home sick, alone—but in another sense, it felt like reading a moving piece of art. It presents less like an autopsy report—how did this marriage die?—and more like an attempt to take a rupture between two people and build a story around that rupture that could recuperate it. The story allows their split to become an indelible part of them both: the origins myth of their ongoing relationship.

After reading the novel, I decided to interview Peter and my mom about how they each remembered the end of their marriage. It was partially that I was curious to see how Peter's perspective had changed with the passage of time, but it was mainly that I wanted to hear my mom's side of the story, too. Peter and I spoke on the phone, always in the afternoon. ("I'm not a morning person," he told me, "as your mom surely remembers.") My mom and I talked across my kitchen table, often with my baby girl napping in the next room—my breast pump wheezing beside my mom's mug of tea, freezer bags of pumped milk between us—as she told me about the woman she'd been before she was my mother.

While Peter's novel portrays Sheila as stoic about the end of her marriage—determined in her resolution to get out, with that firmness in the corner of her mouth—my mom tells me that the months after her separation from Peter were the worst of her life. They split up in November of 1966 and she spent that winter working at a call center, patching calls across the Pacific. Many of the callers were wives and mothers trying to reach soldiers in Saigon or Da Nang, crying over the phone. She can't remember a single one of those calls going through. She started smoking and slept fourteen hours a day. She was attacked in the street one night and almost raped. Her grandmother sent her a copy of her own wedding program with certain phrases underlined from the printed vows: "Till death do us part."

The following summer, my mom went back up to Portland and had a brief affair with her college thesis advisor—out of the feeling that she'd already broken so much in her life, so why not break something else? She looks back now and sees the melodrama of youth in that sentiment, but at the time it seemed clear that she had ruined her life.

If it was slightly disorienting to imagine my mother as the source of Peter's pain, it was far *more* disorienting to imagine her as someone with an outsize narrative of her own. I'd never known her as someone prone to melodrama, had always experienced her—to the contrary—as a force pulling me back from the far ledges of my own melodrama. In the aftermath of every breakup, it had been simultaneously comforting and deflating to hear her say it wasn't the end of the world. Now I realized that wisdom hadn't been entirely intuitive; it had also been a kind of muscle memory—something she might have wanted to tell that version of herself, from the past, the one who thought she'd ruined everything.

Meanwhile, soon after the end of their divorce, Peter got married to another woman in a beautiful beachside ceremony (my mom heard about it from her mother, and felt betrayed that she had gone at all), and they had a baby boy, Shanti. My mom visited them a few weeks after Shanti was born and remembers seeing all three of them lying on a bare mattress in a small apartment. She remembers it was the first time she felt—not just abstractly, but in her gut—the desire for a child.

While it seemed to my mother that Peter was living precisely the life he had imagined for himself, it felt another way to Peter. He remembers that he spent much of the eighteen months after their separation trying to "reclaim" their marriage, repeatedly pushing the boundaries of the friendship she had agreed to. But that wasn't destined to work, he tells me. "You can only turn yourself out so far, to be what another person wants you to be."

Peter wrote the first draft of *The Parting of the Ways* two years after their divorce, as a way of reconciling himself to the loss. At first it was largely a therapeutic exercise. He was also seeing a counselor, taking LSD regularly as a "sacramental substance," and participating in a nude encounter group (who gathered at someone's house to take off their clothes and dig deep into one another's lives). At one point, the group became convinced that Peter's increasing involvement in nonviolence was about sublimating his anger, and they did an experiment—pinning down his arms and legs and whispering insults in his ears in order to draw this anger out. He tells me simply, "It failed."

Peter initially drafted the novel in the first person, to keep its self-analysis explicit and immediate. He compressed and exaggerated certain events to convey the intensity that he had felt while living them, but mainly he tried to stay faithful to what happened. When I ask him why he wrote it, he quotes Nietzsche: "Memory says you did. Pride says you couldn't have. Memory slinks into the background." He didn't want to let memory slink into the background. He didn't want to let his own pride rewrite the truth. "Let me grab hold of this stuff, as honestly as I can," he remembers telling himself. "Put it down so that it can be trapped." It was a way of holding on to my mother, so he could let go of her in life.

Peter eventually settled on a third-person narrative, hoping that a bit more distance might allow it to become something more like art, but then decided that the third person felt cowardly and evasive—so he switched it back. He rewrote the book in the middle of the Oregon woods, west of Salem, where he was helping to set up a commune. He sat at a desk in the communal workroom—surrounded by children and spare triangular tiles meant for an unfinished ellipsoid dome—and tried to bring in imagined first-person perspectives from the other characters, mainly my mother. If he was drawing from her experience, he felt he owed it to her to include her point of view.

When I ask if he was worried that anger would color his portrait of my mother, he insists, "I wasn't angry. Just enormously sad."

The name Sheila feels so alien to my mom that she has sometimes wondered if it was an act of aggression on Peter's part to name her that. I see her point: the name feels too golden, too frolicky, like it belongs to a perky woman in cutoff shorts. But her character in the novel struck me as a recognizable and clearly awestruck portrait—perhaps recognizable *because* it was awestruck. Like mine, Peter's vision of my mother is bent and distorted by a kind of worshipful love.

Sheila is competent, nurturing, and supremely attuned to other people's moods, especially when they are upset or need to be drawn out of themselves. But she is also savvy about where these moods are coming from. At one point, she correctly deduces that Peter is simply *framing* his bad mood as being about his frustration with "authoritarianism," when really he is annoyed that she's not paying more attention to him. This is Peter—as author, years later—recognizing that my mother sometimes knew him better than he knew himself.

But for all her nurturing, Sheila also comes across as disarmingly self-contained. She is constantly seeking space. That's where the firm set in the corner of her mouth comes from. In certain ways, her character is a fantasy of how I've always wanted to be: craving and creating boundaries, rather than trying to dissolve or overrun them. That's part of what Peter loved most about my mom, he tells me: that they were "so much together, but not merging." It was also what allowed her to leave him.

When I ask my mother what she remembers from that summer full of acid trips, lust and intrigue, long nights of weed and scratchy records, she says, "I remember going to the library."

She explains about the Peace Corps: She and Peter had been assigned to Liberia that September, and she wanted to read as much as she could about it before they left. They'd originally been scheduled to leave for Bechuanaland at the beginning of the summer, but Peter had wanted to spend time in Berkeley, living as hippies, so they got reassigned to Liberia for September. In August, he said he didn't want to go to Liberia, so they didn't go anywhere at all. Looking back, my mom can see that Peter never really wanted to go to Africa—it was something he'd told her he was willing to do, or told *himself* he was willing to do, in order to convince her to marry him in the first place.

When we talk about how there are always two sides to every story, we often imagine conflicting accounts of what happened. But more often, I think, the disagreement is about what belongs in the story at all. For my mother, the Peace Corps was a central part of the story of that summer. It was the first thing she wanted to talk about. For Peter, it didn't even show up in his novel. It wasn't the crux of what mattered. His marriage died on another hill entirely.

Besides going to the library, what else does my mother remember from the summer of 1966? Lots of parties. Lots of weed. Lots of acid. Lots of really cheap red wine, much of it drunk in the communal house where she and Peter slept in a living room with a curtained nook. "That nook!" she exclaims. She definitely remembers that nook. "It's where Rob and I went the first night we slept together, while Peter was in the room right next to us." Earl from the novel was really named Rob. He and my mom and Peter all went backpacking together—trying to test the boundaries of openness—and dropped acid high up in the mountains, clambering naked over sparkling granite boulders in the alpine sun. They all got terrible sunburns. (In the novel, Earl's sunburn from that trip is described as "Communist-China red.")

My mom says she was attracted to the risk of taking Rob into that nook, with her husband so close. They had an open marriage, but there was still something electric about the transgression. Looking back, she can see she was trying to break something that she sensed was already ruptured.

When she describes that climactic acid trip at her mother's home, she says it ended in a terrifying attack of claustrophobia. "It makes sense that I met fear on the hill," she tells me. "I was stuck in this place where I couldn't control it. . . . I couldn't believe that it was going to end and I was going to come out of the other side of it."

A few months after reading *The Parting of the Ways*, I fly to Portland to give a reading at Reed, where my mom and Peter first fell in love in the early 1960s. I have invited my mom to fly up from Los Angeles, and Peter to drive in from Salem, so that I can hear the story of their beginning from both of them, together, with the landscape of their shared past as our backdrop.

It's a sunny midwinter day. Peter arrives wearing a leather beret and an oatmeal-colored cardigan sweater with a SAFE PLACE pin. When we sit down at the Reed campus coffeehouse—beside a girl with a fauxhawk reading Foucault and a long-haired guy reading *The Odyssey*—Peter tells me that the students remind him of the people he went to school with. As we walk to my mom's freshman dorm, we pass a cardboard sign inviting people to submit audio recordings of their own orgasms to something called the Gallery of Sexuality. Looking up at my mom's window on the third floor of Ladd Hall, Peter tells me about his own freshman-year roommate—a Muslim from Zanzibar, who brought out his prayer rug five times a day—and their next-door neighbor, who listened to the same Joan Baez album on loop for weeks. Peter knew every note.

They take me downtown to Pioneer Courthouse, where they did their first protest together, against the House Un-American Activities Committee. The twee Portland all around us—full of backyard beehives, bicycle repair shops, and artisanal ice creameries serving flavors like fennel and zucchini—is not the Portland they knew, which felt deeply conservative and parochial. Peter tells me about the woman who balled up one of his flyers and spit on it. Another woman told my mom, "I hope your children grow up to hate you."

Peter sounds protective when he describes the woman who cursed my mom, and my mom remembers liking his protectiveness. One time when she got harassed by a stranger at a march, she noticed the tendons in Peter's neck grow taut from anger because he wanted to hit the guy but was struggling to stay committed to nonviolence. When my mom remembers wanting to impress Peter with her political consciousness, he grins and leans over to touch her leg—so tender, so pleased. When he tells me about his first impression of my mom as "eye candy," I feel like we've landed inside a strange, benevolent mode of triangulated flirtation: it's as if Peter is still flirting with my mom, after all these years, and it's somehow important I am their witness.

My mom and Peter drive me to the empty lot on Lambert Street where their first house once stood. It was where Peter home-brewed beer in a big garbage can in the kitchen and buried three kegs under the floorboards; one exploded. A couple came to dinner one night, and after the meal the wife said, "If it's okay, my husband is going to have dessert"—then he started breast-feeding right there at the table. It sounds like the punch line to a joke: How do you make two aspiring hippies feel like prudes?

My mom points out the building where she got her first birth control pills, and where the doctor shamed her for getting them. They take me to their house on Knapp Street, where they lived after getting married, with a plum tree in the backyard and a walnut tree in the front. My mom cooked lentils with prunes, and Peter scoured the coupon pages to buy potato chips in bulk. My mom wrote her senior thesis about *Havelok the Dane*, a French medieval epic, and Peter got a job as a door-to-door vacuum salesman, then quit after being forced to repossess a vacuum from a single mother with six kids who couldn't make her payments. My mom loved him for that.

Both Peter and my mom agree that she wasn't ready to get married. "Your mother had to be convinced," Peter tells me. She says, "I ran out of reasons to say no."

He met each of her objections—she wanted to travel, to join the Peace Corps, to go to grad school—with a promise: they could do these things together. It was like trying to win a debate in a humanities class, he says. "I shouldn't have talked her into it."

My mom says she was deeply in love with Peter but not ready to be married to anyone. She tells me, "I wish I could have understood that better then."

Peter describes the end of their marriage as the breakdown of a certain youthful faith. "I grew up thinking I could do anything I wanted," he says, "and here was something I *really* wanted and I couldn't make it work."

Hearing this, I get a flash of pride at the fact that Peter wanted to be with my mother more than she wanted to be with him. This pride comes from the same internal place as the delusion I spent much of my young adulthood believing: that it is better to be the one desired more, rather than the one doing more desiring. As if love were a contest; as if desire were fixed, or absolute; as if either position could insulate you from being harmed or causing harm; as if being in control could insulate you from anything.

It's not quite melodrama to say that the world fell apart after Peter and my mom's divorce. The end of the sixties saw the assassinations of Martin Luther King Jr. and Bobby Kennedy, race riots all across the country, billy clubs at the '68 Democratic National Convention, and Nixon's secret treason—all set against the unrelenting heartbreak of bloodshed in Vietnam.

Amid all this, *because* of all this, Peter decided to commit himself fully to formal training in nonviolent resistance. He founded his commune in the Oregon woods. It was meant to be a place where urban activists could come for a few months to decompress in the wake of major actions.

After my mom pulled out of her depression, she met Lucy, her next serious romance, and then traveled to London to be with my aunt, who was pregnant at nineteen. Eventually my mom and Lucy went to follow the crop season in southern France, even organizing a strike among their fellow olive pickers to protest long workdays in the cold. Back in the States, once their relationship had ended, my mom fell in love with a young professor of economics at Stanford: my father. They moved into a house on campus, and within the next two years, she'd have two sons—my older brothers.

Two roads diverged in a wood: one led to a commune, and the other led to faculty housing.

My mother has been married three times. After Peter, her marriage to my father lasted twenty-three years and ended when I was eleven. He was exciting, successful, and as she always told me, "never boring." He was also chronically unfaithful, and often out of town. After I left for college, she met Walter, a retired ketchup salesman, through their social justice work in the Episcopal Church. They became grandparents together and marched through the streets to protest the second war in Iraq. The stories I told myself about these three marriages eventually distilled into three primal male archetypes: the brash, idealistic young dreamer; the restless, intoxicating, difficult soul mate;

and the stable partner to settle down with after all the drama was done. I clung to this distillation.

Perhaps it's no surprise, then, that part of what I found fascinating about *The Parting of the Ways* was its portrayal of Peter as a character navigating various archetypes of masculinity—the "straight" man, the cool man, the lover, the protector, the provider, the protester—and trying to find his place among them. He constructs his character with an endearing awareness of his own fumbling, his contradictions: he's the guy who gets high at a dinner party and pretends to be King Arthur, pulling a knife out of a stick of butter—but he's also the guy who whispers to two strangers sharing a needle to shoot speed, "Haven't you ever heard of hepatitis?" While Peter the character falls into long-winded monologues about his quest to discover himself, Peter the author gently pokes fun at his pretensions—having another character, at one point, doze off during one of his rants. But Peter's obsession with coolness, and later, his interrogation of that obsession, are really expressions of a deeper and more universal hunger: the fantasy of an utterly authentic self, unfettered by norms, absolutely free.

My mom remembers being frustrated that Peter didn't want to go to graduate school, and telling him that she didn't think he had the rigor to handle it. "He did, of course," she tells me. "And it's an unfair thing to do with anyone, to lash out like that—it was an expression of my frustration that he wasn't using his gifts to live the kind of life that I wanted to lead."

It's eerie to hear my mom talk about her disappointment at the ways Peter didn't live up to the ambitions she'd projected onto him, because it reminds me so fully of the ways I have projected ambitions onto my own partners for years. It hasn't been ego extension so much as a desire to dwell in states of awe—to feel inspired and somehow bettered—but it can also feel like callousness, or distance. It feels like company to hear my mom articulating her own version of it.

My mom tells me she hopes Peter doesn't remember their hard conversation about graduate school. I remind her there's a version of it in the novel. But while my mom mainly regrets the cruelty of her comments, Peter's version of the conversation is more focused on his anger in response: "My voice is not loud, but there is so much violence in it that Sheila is stunned for a moment. I pause for several heartbeats, savoring the drama of the situation, savoring the feeling of power." Both Peter and my mom remember being the one who inflicted pain.

When my mom tells me about a revelation she had during one of their acid trips that summer—realizing that her father was never going to be a world-famous engineer, that her outsize sense of his importance didn't match his standing in the world—I can't help but think her feelings about her father shaped her desire for Peter to pursue a kind of worldly success and her eventual marriage to my dad, just as my feelings about my father have shaped my own ambitions and the ways I have sought ambition in my partners, or projected my ambitions onto them.

Peter never went to graduate school. "The commune was my

graduate school," he tells me. He learned how to take care of whatever needed taking care of. At one point, when they desperately needed money, a nearby farmer offered to pay Peter to help him get his chickens off to slaughter. There were thousands of them. At first, Peter imagined he would carefully cradle each chicken in his palms, treating them with dignity and compassion. But by the end, he'd started to handle them more like troublemakers. He understood how prison wardens might feel. As hard as we try to fight the structures we find ourselves inside of, we are all still shaped by them. At a certain point, in all their *bawk-bawk-bawk*ing, he started to hear the animals calling his own name.

My mother and Peter finally saw each other again near the end of their twenties. He came to visit her at Stanford, on his way from the commune to see his parents in Southern California. My mom doesn't remember it as a happy reunion. Peter made it clear he thought she had betrayed all their young values. A *business school professor*? When I ask whether Peter made his judgment explicit, or if she could just sense it, she tells me, "He made it pretty explicit." He gave her a hard time about having a dishwasher. What could be more bourgeoisie?

As she tells me this, I think of how Sheila is always in the kitchen of their communal house in Peter's novel—making a beef stew, or a Jell-O dessert, or dream bars. Even during their years of free love, *someone* had been doing the dishes. Now she just had a dishwasher. I feel defensive on her behalf.

When I ask if she felt misunderstood by Peter, she shakes her head. "I didn't feel misunderstood. Just hurt. Back then I didn't have a plan for everything that would happen later."

It wasn't that she envied Peter's life on the commune. In fact, he had a habit of telling people what to do—and how to do it—and she could imagine that it might get a bit tiring to live in a commune that he'd founded. But at least his life had a certain clarity, an unmistakable moral urgency. Perhaps the specter of unlived lives—the life with Peter, or the one he was living without her—held even more force because her own life was still coming into focus. Perhaps I project false confidence onto my younger mother because it's uncomfortable for me to imagine her in terms of uncertainty. For me, she has always been the source of inviolable love, the definition of devotion, the absence of contingency.

How does Peter remember that Palo Alto visit? At first, he simply echoes my mom's sentiments. It was uncomfortable. He didn't like my father, but it was hard for him to untangle whether it actually had to do with him or the fact that he'd ended up with my mom. But when I ask Peter whether he remembered judging my mother, whether he'd really thought she had betrayed the shared ideals of their youth, he pauses for a long time. "Okay," he says finally. "She did a very strange thing at that meeting. We never talked about it, and it still mystifies me."

He tells me that she came out in a very sheer negligee as she introduced him to her new husband. Peter couldn't understand what she was trying to communicate. For years, he would have killed to see her come out in that negligee. For years, he had been waiting for some sign from her that maybe there was hope between them. But at that point, he didn't know what to do with it. My mom has no memory of wearing that negligee. She doesn't remember trying to send him any signs at all—though it's also true we don't always remember the signs we once tried to send, or weren't even aware of trying to send them in the moment.

"Did I see her as selling out?" he says. "Maybe a little bit."

He looked at her new husband, my father, and thought, He's a Stanford professor, he's got two PhDs, he's good-looking. My dad only has one PhD, but it makes sense that Peter exaggerated his status in memory. It felt to Peter as if my mom was saying, See how much better I'm doing now; I've moved way up the ladder from you. Peter found himself thinking, What do I have that he doesn't have? The answer was conviction: fidelity to the set of values he and my mom had shared.

Although Peter and my mom have both stayed committed to the ideals that brought them together in the first place, Peter's commitment has meant working outside institutions, or against them, while my mother has worked within them: the academy, the nonprofit, the church. Peter has spent the past fifty years as a nonviolent resister and a tax protestor, playing guitar in a political satire band called Dr. Atomic's Medicine Show. His son, Shanti—the baby my mother saw on the mattress, years ago, who was raised on the commune—has become a corporate executive.

Over those same fifty years, my mother not only married an economics professor but became a professor herself, of public health, and raised three kids while doing PhD fieldwork on infant malnutrition in rural Brazil, bringing two young sons to rural villages where she was weighing malnourished babies on hammock scales, and spending decades researching maternal health in West Africa. Her version of retirement involved becoming an Episcopal deacon and running after-school nutrition programs for kids from low-income communities through the church.

Both of their lives can make you feel exhausted, and more than a little bit guilty, like, *What have I done to save the world today?* They've both gotten arrested plenty of times, protesting wars and wage gaps and nuclear force, but my mother has done it in clerical robes, usually returning from jail to find a text message from her daughter waiting on her cell phone.

After fifty years, their intimacy holds so much friction and rupture and youth. Intimacy after a divorce might not come cheaply, but it runs deep. It runs deeper for its price. It's about knowing who someone was and how they changed—and carrying all those past versions of them inside. More than once, Peter tells me, "Despite all my other relationships, I have never stopped loving your mother."

In Portland, after our visit to the house on Knapp Street, we head to a protest at the Army Corps of Engineers. Peter is carrying two flags: a peace flag and an Earth flag. It's February, at the tail end of the Standing Rock protest against an oil pipeline proposed to run under the Missouri River, near Native lands. At this point, most of the water protectors have already left, and the rest will be cleared later that month. The Army Corps of Engineers has granted permission for the pipe to get laid. That's what we are protesting.

Turns out that the offices of the Army Corps of Engineers are located in a very staid office building behind a shopping mall, across from a small homeless encampment. But we don't see a protest anywhere: not in the parking lot outside the office building, not in the lobby itself. We just see a single security guard behind a desk. He asks us politely, "Can I help you?"

I am embarrassed. I feel absurd. But Peter asks the security guard where we can find the Army Corps of Engineers. He directs us to the fourth floor.

Part of me is expecting to find a very small protest on the fourth floor, but there is no very small protest on the fourth floor—or else, we *are* the very small protest on the fourth floor. There's just a friendly receptionist behind a desk. When the other elevator opens, we see the security guard from the lobby.

"I decided I'd follow you up," he says. "You all looked confused."

"We *are* confused," Peter tells him. "We also have a message for the Army Corps of Engineers."

On my own, I'd already be out the door—probably partially relieved that the protest wasn't happening, that we could spend the next few hours talking instead; probably suggesting we all get coffee. But Peter tells the receptionist, "We'd like to speak to someone about what's happening at Standing Rock."

She asks us to wait and then disappears into a warren of cubicles. A few moments later, to my great surprise, a colonel in full fatigues comes out to the reception area and invites us back. He is calling our bluff. But that's the thing: Peter isn't bluffing. This is him in action—no awkwardness, all persistence.

The colonel ends up taking us to a glass-walled conference room, where he sits at the head of a long oval table. Peter sits next to him, propping his peace flag and his Earth flag on the leather swivel seat beside him as if they are obedient children. Later, the internet will tell me that this colonel spent time in both Iraq and Afghanistan. Close up, his fatigues are impressive, their canvas creases crisp and imposing.

We are joined by a much younger man wearing a sage-green fleece vest. "This is Jason," says the colonel. "He's one of our lawyers." Jason gives us a sheepish smile.

Peter launches into an articulate, passionate, and surprisingly specific account of what concerns him about the pipeline being laid near the Standing Rock reservation. When Jason launches into a technical reply, the colonel cuts him off. "Too many acronyms!" he says. "Sounds like alphabet soup."

Then the colonel takes a piece of blank paper and starts drawing a map: the Missouri River, the "existing easement," the Standing Rock tribal lands. It's not like the Army Corps of Engineers is *building* the pipeline, he reminds us. They are just granting permission. My mom brings up an order issued by Obama that got overturned. Peter backs her up; he seems to know every court order that has ever been at play. I stay silent. I'm impressed by Peter and my mother's knowledge, and also relieved by it. I'd expected a regular protest—where I could chant in relative ignorance, self-satisfied and anonymous—but this is something else: a kind of pop quiz. What do I actually know about Standing Rock? Not enough to talk to a colonel for an hour.

As the conversation continues, it's clear that the lawyer and the colonel are coming from different places: while the colonel is a company man, toeing the line completely, Jason comes across as deeply troubled. He went to law school to study tribal law. Maybe he started working here so that he could reform the system from the inside out. Or at least, that's the story I've written for him in my head. Now he's sitting in a corporate office in a fleece vest defending a pipeline through tribal lands. He seems quietly heartbroken. The colonel's stance is more like, What do you want me to do about it? He seems exasperated by our constant questions about "their land." At one point, he raises his voice: "We're all on their land, right here! Everything is their land!"

At this, Peter and I share a knowing glance: *Exactly.*

The colonel tells us that the Army Corps has gone "above and beyond" consulting with the tribe. They've done their due diligence. This is when I finally work up the nerve to say something. "Well, the tribe seems to disagree."

Peter chimes in: "Along with three hundred other tribes!"

Jason keeps bringing us back to the Sioux Treaty of 1868 and the precedent it set. "You might have whatever feelings you have about the Treaty of 1868," he says, "and I might have whatever feelings I have about the Treaty of 1868—"

I cut him off: "What feelings do you have about the Treaty of 1868?"

He says, "It was a tragedy."

A few beats of silence pass. We all hold that truth. I keep waiting for Jason and the colonel to check their watches. The colonel repeats that they have adhered to every law. "I don't think you guys are breaking any laws," I say. "I think the laws are broken."

It sounds smug and self-righteous the moment I say it, as if I'm plagiarizing from a documentary about sixties activism, but when Peter says, "Yes!" I flush with pride. I'm pleased that I've impressed him, the radical activist, and also aware that I'm enacting and replicating my mother's own desires from years ago: to be good enough for him.

All told, we meet with Jason and the colonel for almost an hour and a half in their glass-walled conference room on "their land." I spend much of the time confused about why we haven't yet been politely escorted to the door. Is this a PR thing? A Portland thing? Don't they have work to do?

Just before we leave, Peter calls upon both men to look deep into themselves and think about what they believe is right. Maybe it's cheesy, but a voice in me is also saying, Amen!

As we walk out of the office, I can hear my mother inviting Jason to my reading that evening. Mothers will still be mothers, even in the offices of the Army Corps of Engineers.

By the time we reach the parking lot, I'm already fantasizing about how this conversation might change the entire course of Jason's career, and once we get to the car, my mother confesses that she has been having exactly the same daydream: five years from now, he will look back on today as the day that changed his life. My ego and my mother's ego are built in similar ways. Once again, I search for the edges between us, try to remind myself they are there. But there is a kind of amniotic pleasure in having trouble locating these edges, in feeling this symmetry instead, this union. How had Peter put it? *So much together, but not merging.* Sometimes it feels good to merge, to say—irrationally, feverishly, stubbornly—*I am my mother, and she is me.*

Jason and the colonel must have assumed we were a family: two tall ex-hippies in their early seventies and their tall daughter. And today, in a strange way, we are: the manifestation of an alternate reality, the road not traveled, in which Peter and my mom had a child together, and took her with them—three decades later—to keep protesting the world.

Whenever I locate differences between me and my mom, I mainly construct them as self-punishing binaries: She studied malnourished children. I had an eating disorder. She left her marriage with stoic fortitude. My ex-boyfriend once called me a wound dweller.

While I'm preoccupied by my own pain, she is preoccupied by the pain of others. Or maybe she isn't preoccupied by pain at all, but by strategies of subsistence and survival.

For years, though I never articulated it explicitly to myself, I suspected that my only choices were to identify with my mom completely or else to somehow fail her. When I read *The Parting of the Ways*, I found myself either projecting onto her character or else shaming myself with the gaps between us: her stoicism, my woundedness; her outwardness, my self-concern. She was unhappy in her relationship because she wanted to show up for her Peace Corps assignment. I was unhappy in my last relationship because I wanted more frequent text messages. I connected more to Peter's "wriggling eel of pain" than I did to her firm-set mouth.

It's also true, however, that I've been the one to leave almost every relationship I've ever been in—and often, not always, because I felt a certain kind of claustrophobia, which isn't to pathologize my past so much as to suggest that perhaps I share my mom's attachment to distances and boundaries more than I've recognized, that her hunger for independence isn't so alien to me.

When I told Peter this essay would be about his evolving relationship to my mother, it was the truth. But it wasn't all of the truth. Because the essay is also about *my* evolving relationship with my mother, how some part of me wanted to humanize her myth, and how I found, in Peter's portrait of her, another gaze saturated by worship—but also the puncturing of that worship with the admission of her actual, textured self.

I didn't ask Peter's novel to disrupt the stories I told myself about my mom and me, but it did. It allowed me to see that both she and I have always been more complicated than the binaries I've constructed for us to inhabit, in which we are either identical or opposite. We get so used to the stories we tell about ourselves. This is why we sometimes need to find ourselves in the stories of others.

That night in Portland, in the upstairs chapel on the Reed campus where my mom and Peter had once taken their freshman humanities lecture, I read from an essay about the massive women's march that had happened after Trump's inauguration. It was an essay about protest and why it still mattered, even— or especially—as the president seemed to threaten every single value my mom and Peter had spent the past five decades fighting for.

Jason the lawyer had not come to my reading, but my mom and Peter sat side by side in pews near the front—just as they'd sat in those pews years before. It felt like I was speaking to the people they'd once been, when they were protesting at the courthouse downtown and that woman told my mother she hoped her children grew up to hate her, and then when Peter visited my mother in Palo Alto years later, and she worried that she'd disappointed him. That reading was a way of telling her, *You did not disappoint anyone.* It was a way of saying, *Your children will grow up to love you.* It was as if I was trying to project my admiration back through time to reassure the woman my mom had been, that woman who felt only that she had somehow failed the man who loved her first—that woman who did not know, could not have known, the road ahead.

Acknowledgments

Thank you to all fourteen writers featured in this book for sharing such personal and heartfelt stories from their own lives.

An anthology is a collaborative project, and I couldn't have edited this book without the guidance of my whip-smart editor, Karyn Marcus, and my badass agent, Melissa Flashman. Thank you to Taylor Larsen for "locking" me in her parent's dining room so I could finally finish the essay that inspired this book, and to Lauren LeBlanc for her insightful feedback and edits. Thanks to Sari Botton for believing in me and publishing my essay on *Longreads*. Thank you to Gary Filgate and Alison Magill for giving me a home when I really needed one. Thank you to Alisson Wood for being such a supportive friend.

Thanks to the entire team at Simon & Schuster, including Molly Gregory, Kayley Hoffman, Madeline Schmitz, Elise Ringo, and Max Meltzer.

I would be remiss if I didn't thank everyone who helped me shape my essay or encouraged me along the way, including Kelly McMasters, Margot Kahn, Tobias Carroll, Jo Ann Beard and Team Jo Ann Beard at the Tin House Summer Workshop, Jennifer Pastiloff, Lidia Yuknavitch, Caroline Leavitt, Porochista Khakpour, Tom Holbrook, Julia Fierro, Julie Buntin, Brian Chait, and Bethanne Patrick.

Thank you to other anthology editors for their advice: Jennifer Baker, Brian Gresko, Sari Botton, and Lilly Dancyger.

Thank you to my family, including my siblings: Jennifer, Colin, and Emma. Thank you to Michael Filgate and Nancy. Thank you to Leesa.

This book is dedicated to my grandmothers. Nana and Mimo are the strongest women I know.

Thank you to Melissa Wacks for her astute guidance throughout the entire process of working on this book.

And last but certainly not least: Thank you to Sean Fitzroy for making me laugh and being such a wonderful human being. I love you.

About the Authors

André Aciman is a Distinguished Professor of Comparative Literature at the Graduate Center, CUNY. He is the author of *Out of Egypt: A Memoir, False Papers: Essays on Exile and Memory, Alibis: Essays on Elsewhere*, and four novels: *Call Me by Your Name, Eight White Nights, Harvard Square*, and *Enigma Variations*. He is currently working on a novel and a collection of essays. His novel *Call Me by Your Name* was released as a film and was awarded an Oscar for Best Adapted Screenplay in 2018.

Julianna Baggott is the author of more than twenty novels, published under her own name as well as pen names. Her recent novels *Pure* (an ALA Alex Award winner) and *Harriet Wolf's*

Seventh Book of Wonders were *New York Times* Notable Books of the Year. She's published four collections of poetry and her essays have appeared in the *Washington Post*, the *Boston Globe*, the *New York Times* Modern Love column, and on NPR's *Talk of the Nation*, *All Things Considered*, and *Here and Now*. She teaches screenwriting at Florida State University's College of Motion Picture Arts and currently lives in Delaware.

Sari Botton is a writer living in Kingston, New York. She is the essays editor for *Longreads* and editor of the award-winning anthology *Goodbye to All That: Writers on Loving and Leaving New York* and its *New York Times* bestselling follow-up, *Never Can Say Goodbye: Writers on Their Unshakable Love for New York*. She is also the operator of the Kingston Writers' Studio.

Alexander Chee is the bestselling author of the novels *Edinburgh* and *The Queen of the Night*, and *How to Write an Autobiographical Novel*, an essay collection. He is the winner of a Whiting Award and fellowships from the NEA and the MCCA, and his essays and stories have appeared recently in the *New York Times Magazine*, *The Yale Review*, *T* magazine, and *Tin House*. He teaches creative writing at Dartmouth College.

Melissa Febos is the author of the memoir *Whip Smart* and the essay collection *Abandon Me*, which was a Lambda Literary Award finalist, a Publishing Triangle Award finalist, an Indie

Next Pick, and widely named a Best Book of 2017. Febos is the inaugural winner of the Jeanne Córdova Award for Lesbian/ Queer Nonfiction from Lambda Literary and the recipient of the 2017 Sarah Verdone Writing Award from the Lower Manhattan Cultural Council. She has been awarded fellowships from the MacDowell Colony, Bread Loaf Writers' Conference, Virginia Center for the Creative Arts, Vermont Studio Center, the Barbara Deming Memorial Fund, the BAU Institute, and Ragdale. Her essays have recently appeared in *Tin House*, *Granta*, *The Believer*, and the *New York Times*. She lives in Brooklyn.

Michele Filgate's work has appeared in *Longreads*, the *Washington Post*, the *Los Angeles Times*, the *Boston Globe*, *The Paris Review* Daily, *Tin House*, *Gulf Coast*, *O: The Oprah Magazine*, *BuzzFeed*, *Refinery29*, and many other publications. Currently she is an MFA student at NYU, where she is the recipient of the Stein Fellowship. She's a contributing editor at *Literary Hub*, teaches at Catapult and the Sackett Street Writers' Workshop, and has been an instructor at Stanford Continuing Studies and NYU. *What My Mother and I Don't Talk About* is her first book.

Cathi Hanauer is the *New York Times* bestselling author of three novels—*Gone*, *Sweet Ruin*, and *My Sister's Bones*—and two anthologies, *The Bitch in the House* and *The Bitch Is Back*, which was an NPR Best Book of 2016. She's written articles, essays, and criticism for the *New York Times*, *Elle*, *O, the Oprah Magazine*, along with her husband, Daniel Jones, of the *New York Times* Modern Love column. Find her at www.cathihanauer.com.

Leslie Jamison is the author of the *New York Times* bestsellers *The Recovering* and *The Empathy Exams*, as well as a novel, *The Gin Closet*, which was a finalist for the Los Angeles Times Book Prize Art Seidenbaum Award for First Fiction. She is a contributing writer for the *New York Times Magazine*, and her work has appeared in *Harper's Bazaar*, the *Atlantic*, *Oxford American*, and the *Virginia Quarterly Review*, where she is an editor at large. She directs the graduate nonfiction program at Columbia University and lives in Brooklyn with her family.

Dylan Landis is the author of a collection of linked stories, *Normal People Don't Live Like This*, and a novel, *Rainey Royal*. Her stories have appeared in the O. Henry Prize Stories and Best American Nonrequired Reading series, and her essays in the *New York Times Book Review* and *Harper's*. She has received a fellowship in fiction from the National Endowment for the Arts.

Kiese Laymon is the author of *Heavy: An American Memoir*, *How to Slowly Kill Yourself and Others in America*, and *Long Division*. He is also a professor of English and creative writing at the University of Mississippi.

Carmen Maria Machado's debut short story collection, *Her Body and Other Parties*, was a finalist for the National Book

Award, the Kirkus Prize, the Los Angeles Times Book Prize Art Seidenbaum Award for First Fiction, a World Fantasy Award, the International Dylan Thomas Prize, and the PEN/Robert W. Bingham Prize for Debut Fiction, and was the winner of the Bard Fiction Prize, the Lambda Literary Award for Lesbian Fiction, the Brooklyn Public Library Literary Prize, a Shirley Jackson Award, and the National Book Critics Circle's John Leonard Award. In 2018, the *New York Times* listed *Her Body and Other Parties* as a member of "The New Vanguard," one of "Fifteen remarkable books by women that are shaping the way we read and write fiction in the twenty-first century." Her essays, fiction, and criticism have appeared in the *New Yorker*, the *New York Times*, *Granta*, *Harper's Bazaar*, *Tin House*, *Virginia Quarterly Review*, *Timothy McSweeney's Quarterly Concern*, *The Believer*, *Guernica*, Best American Science Fiction and Fantasy, Best American Nonrequired Reading, and elsewhere. She is the writer in residence at the University of Pennsylvania and lives in Philadelphia with her wife.

Bernice L. McFadden is the author of nine critically acclaimed novels, including *Sugar*, *Loving Donovan*, *Nowhere Is a Place*, *The Warmest December*, *Gathering of Waters* (a *New York Times* Editors' Choice and one of the 100 Notable Books of 2012), *Glorious*, and *The Book of Harlan* (winner of a 2017 American Book Award and the NAACP Image Award for Outstanding Literary Work, Fiction). She is a four-time Hurston/Wright Legacy Award finalist, as well as the recipient of three awards from the Black

Caucus of the American Library Association (BCALA). *Praise Song for the Butterflies* is her latest novel.

Nayomi Munaweera is the award-winning author of the novels *Island of a Thousand Mirrors* and *What Lies Between Us.* The *Huffington Post* has said, "Munaweera's prose is visceral and indelible, devastatingly beautiful—reminiscent of the glorious writings of Louise Erdrich, Amy Tan, and Alice Walker, who also find ways to truth-tell through fiction." The *New York Times Book Review* called her first novel "incandescent." She wants you to know that the essay in this book is the hardest thing she's written yet.

Lynn Steger Strong is the author of the novel *Hold Still.* Her nonfiction has appeared in *Guernica, Los Angeles Review of Books, Elle, Catapult,* and elsewhere. She teaches writing at Columbia University, Fairfield University, and the Pratt Institute.

Brandon Taylor is a student at the Iowa Writers' Workshop in fiction. His debut novel is forthcoming from Riverhead Books.

Permissions

Introduction copyright © 2019 and "What My Mother and I Don't Talk About" copyright © 2019 by Michele Filgate

"My Mother's (Gate) Keeper" copyright © 2019 by Cathi Hanauer

"Thesmophoria" copyright © 2019 by Melissa Febos

"Xanadu" copyright © 2019 by Alexander Chee

"16 Minetta Lane" copyright © 2019 by Dylan Landis

"Fifteen" copyright © 2019 by Bernice L. McFadden

"Nothing Left Unsaid" copyright © 2019 by Julianna Baggott

"The Same Story About My Mom" copyright © 2019 by Lynn Steger Strong

"While These Things / Feel American to Me" copyright © 2019 by Kiese Laymon

"Mother Tongue" copyright © 2019 by Carmen Maria Machado

"Are You Listening?" copyright © 2014 by André Aciman

"Brother, Can You Spare Some Change?" copyright © 2019 by Sari Botton

"Her Body / My Body" copyright © 2019 by Nayomi Munaweera

"All About My Mother" copyright © 2018 by Brandon Taylor

"I Met Fear on the Hill" copyright © 2019 by Leslie Jamison

The following stories were reprinted with permission:

"What My Mother and I Don't Talk About" was previously published on *Longreads* on October 9, 2017

"All About My Mother" was previously published on Lit Hub on August 1, 2018

"Are You Listening" was previously published in *The New Yorker* on March 17, 2014

About the Editor

© SYLVIE ROSOKOFF

Michele Filgate's work has appeared in *Longreads*, the *Washington Post*, the *Los Angeles Times*, the *Boston Globe*, *The Paris Review* Daily, *Tin House*, *Gulf Coast*, *O: The Oprah Magazine*, *BuzzFeed*, *Refinery29*, and many other publications. Currently she is an MFA student at NYU, where she is the recipient of the Stein Fellowship. She's a contributing editor at *Literary Hub*, teaches at Catapult and the Sackett Street Writers' Workshop, and has been an instructor at Stanford Continuing Studies and NYU. *What My Mother and I Don't Talk About* is her first book.